MEMOIRS OF A FORTUNATE LIFE

The Evolution of an Activist

SARAI G. ZITTER

PublishAmerica
Baltimore

First printing

PublishAmerica has allowed this work to remain exactly as the author intended, verbatim, without editorial input.

Softcover 9781462646876
PUBLISHED BY PUBLISHAMERICA, LLLP
www.publishamerica.com
Baltimore

Printed in the United States of America

DEDICATION

This book is for my children, each of whom is working to build a better world, and for my grandchildren, my bridge to the future. It is dedicated to the memories of my mother, my role model and mentor, and of Sam, who made it all worthwhile.

For Helene—
Whose love and friendship have been among the sustaining forces of my life!
Love,
Sarah

PREFACE

Dorothy Parker once wrote:

"When you come to this time of abatement,
To this passage from summer to fall,
It is manners to issue a statement
As to what you got out of it all."

It is in this spirit that, at the age of eighty-four and with the encouragement of my children, I am putting pen to paper (or fingers to computer) to write what we may grandiosely call my "memoirs." In a way, this is a gift to my grandchildren. Just as they will live much of their lives in a world I shall never know, so have I evolved in a past they cannot see, but in which perhaps they will have some interest. And as my cousin Judi has long urged me to write a book on child-rearing, I may throw in some of that philosophy as well.

Many incidents from my past have already been written in essay form, either for my own pleasure, for a class, or for publication in my community news magazine. I shall probably save time and effort by including some of these verbatim. And of course, I'll try to include family stories that my children have enjoyed throughout the years.

MEMOIRS OF A FORTUNATE LIFE

The Evolution of an Activist

CHAPTER I: THE EARLY YEARS

I was born in 1926, in a private home in the East Bronx. I was in a great hurry to see the world; after a week or so of false labor, I came so quickly that my mother did not have time to go to the hospital. She, with her foster-sister Anne, was making ice cream when labor began, and she barely had time to get to her bed when I arrived. My physician-father got home just in time to tie off the cord. (Can Mother's ice-cream making be blamed for my ever-ready sweet tooth?)

According to my mother, I was a beautiful baby, with pink cheeks and "a cap of golden curls". I might have thought that was simply maternal hype, until I heard her describe my brother, born at 22 inches long, as arriving "looking like a drowned rat". He was two years my senior, with a birthday just three days after mine. He was told that I was a very special birthday present, and he must take really good care of me. He has been claiming to do so ever since.

It wasn't always easy. There were the many times when I would walk past where he was building with blocks; my foot would shoot out as I strolled by, and down would go the edifice. But it wasn't a one-way street. Mother recalled my coming to her, crying; Barry and his friends were playing Cowboys and Indians, and they wanted me to be the cow. Then there was the time I somehow became a prisoner, and Barry heaved a brick at me when I attempted to escape. My scalp still bears the scar!

Mostly, however, Barry was kinder to me than are most big brothers, and he showed his kindness in ways both great and small. For my sixth birthday, he not only gave me the two-wheeler bike he had outgrown, but also taught me to ride. (As I recall, he then bought himself a third-hand bike from a neighbor, paying the munificent sum of $2.50 out of his own allowance.) He was my companion in ice-skating, and my partner in rowing from the time that we sat side by side on the rowboat's seat, each handling one oar. Later, we took ballroom dancing lessons together; I still remember practicing the Lindy-Hop to the strains of "Old John Silver" on our wind-up victrola. So Barry gets partial credit for my lifelong love of dancing. Many years later, he even taught me to drive.

Music was very important in our family. My father had a fine baritone voice, and with his siblings formed quite a good family quartet. They knew all the popular songs and show tunes of the time, so that my own song repertoire goes back for several decades before I was born. Among my favorite memories are the Sunday nights when we all stood around the piano, played by Barry, and sang together. I suspect that my antipathy towards television began when my father started watching it on Sunday nights, so that the heart went out of our musical evenings.

Mother always loved New York City and the many venues and activities it provided. We went to all the places that usually attract only tourists, places like the Empire State Building and the Statue of Liberty. We went to museums – my favorites were the Museum of Natural History and the wonderfully interactive Museum of Science and Industry. And we went to concerts! At the Earnest Schilling Children's Concerts, given by the Metropolitan Orchestra, I became entranced by the harp. Mother insisted that each of us begin our musical education with two years of piano, after which we were free to continue, to switch to another instrument, or – horrors! – to give up music lessons altogether. At age nine I was permitted to switch to the harp, and I continued with lessons until I went off to college.

It was 1935 when I began studying the harp – the depths of the depression. I later learned that my harp was the only thing my frugal parents ever bought 'on time' in the fifty-eight years of their marriage. (Many years later, when my daughter Robin took up the harp, someone asked what had made her think of it. I replied, "Oh, there just happened to be one around the house!")

Perhaps they made that financial stretch in part because they thought I needed extra emotional support. I had spoken with a stammer since age two, when I had the mastoid operation which left me permanently deaf in my right ear. (This was before the days of antibiotics. When my niece, Ruthie, began to show the same chronic ear infections which had preceded my surgery, sulfa drugs were available, making the outcome very different indeed.) To such an articulate child as I, stammering was a handicap indeed, and perhaps my parents felt that playing an unusual instrument such as the harp would help me to develop the self-confidence that every child needs.

Poetry was also an important family theme, particularly so for my mother and me. Mother had the gift of easy memorizing and seemingly endless recollection, and that is a gift which I share. (I enjoy seeing the gift passed on particularly to my son, and am getting glimmers that it continues in the next generation). I also wrote little verses – I hesitate to dignify them with the name of poetry – and Mother kept a notebook of my juvenile compositions. She once told me of the book that, as a child, she had started of her own works. It was grandiloquently titled "The Complete Works of Rose Sigal".

Sarai G. Zitter

I began at age three or four with such works as:

See the little drops of rain
Crying down the window pane.
Pitter-patter. Pitter-patter.
The sky is crying; what's the matter?

Progressed through:

Let it rain!
I don't mind!
There's a book I can find.

I'm alone
All the day?
Here's a book, keeps me gay.

Brother's cross?
Let him be.
Just a book pleases me.

And by 12 or so had developed a bit more sophistication
(even a title!) with:

AUTUMN COLORS
Scarlet and gold, the autumn leaves
Crackle beneath my feet.
The dark brown earth feels pleasant, as I
Walk with footsteps fleet
Under a yellow sun
Whose warmth has just begun.

Many greens, both light and dark,
The hillside brings to view.
The deep blue of the river

Reflects the sky's clear blue.
Coming home, a purple haze
Has settled on the Palisades.

Alas, the notebook has been lost, and through the years my creative poetry has been limited to greeting cards, deliberately purchased without verses so that I might supply my own. Again, this versifying skill has developed, to an extent far superior to my own, in my daughter Sherry.

The ability to retain memorized poetry and songs has provided great satisfaction throughout my life. As my father's memory slipped, he would read the words of songs off my lips as we were singing. My brother, also a poetry-lover, still finds it easier to ask me for the correct wording of a poem or quote, than to look it up. And to this day, when I go to bed I mentally recite poetry to put myself to sleep.

I recall using this skill at Girl Scout camp, when we had a 'country fair', and were encouraged to have individual booths. My contribution was an Instant Verse booth; I would write an immediate quatrain on any subject the 'purchaser' selected. I felt a bit guilty at how impressed people often were with this skill; to me, it seemed so easy.

When I was in seventh grade, we were assigned to memorize ten lines of Longfellow's "Evangeline", and be prepared to recite it to the class on the following day. I memorized the prologue, several verses into the body of the poem, the description of Evangeline (which Mother told me was a particularly famous portion) and then, thinking that the teacher might want exactly ten lines, added in a precisely ten-line bit from elsewhere in the book.

11

This done, I set to work helping my next-door neighbor and friend, Edith, with her own memorizing. I think it was at that moment in time that I first became aware of the significance of some of the innate differences among human beings. Edith worked far harder at her school work than did I. Her diligence paid off with good grades, too. But memorizing ten lines of poetry was almost beyond her. I drilled her; I taught her some of the 'tricks' I found helpful; we went over her lines again and again. But when it came time to recite them the next day, she - who had poured such effort into this assignment – stumbled through her ten lines with difficulty, while I – who had breezed through extensive memorization - got kudos for my performance. It wasn't fair! That may have been one of the first times that I was conscious of my many blessings.

I have no recollection of the house in which I was born, but was once shown the only wall left standing, then used as a billboard, on Washington Avenue and 175th street. I was four when the house was sold and my family moved to an apartment at 240 East 176th Street. I can't visualize the apartment, but I do remember being on the roof with Mother as she was hanging up our wet clothes. In those days nobody had a washing machine. We 'sent out' the laundry, and received it back either as 'wet wash' or 'flat wash'. The wet wash was just that – the laundered, wet clothing was delivered in a heavy cloth sack, and we hung it to dry on lines on the roof. The flat wash was the bed linens, which came back ironed, folded and ready for use.

We also sent Dad's shirts to the Chinese hand laundry – I believe we paid thirteen cents apiece. The only time in my entire life that I ever heard Mother say, "Don't tell Dad", was a day during the Depression, when he came home early. To save those thirteen cents, Mother was washing and ironing his shirts herself– but she never told him. So she slid the drainboard back over the kitchen tub full of soapy shirts, and went to greet him as usual.

Another Depression tid-bit – there was a three-cent deposit on the glass bottles in which we bought cream. When there were two or three of them collected under the sink, my mother would sometimes suggest that I bring them back to the store – and I was allowed to keep the money. Thus my early ten-cent allowance might be doubled, and even when it was raised to 25 cents, that extra six or nine pennies came in very handy.

We lived on 176th Street for only two years, and then moved to 1690 Weeks Avenue, just a couple of blocks from the building on the Grand Concourse where my father had his professional office. By that time, he was specializing in pediatrics. He had been in general practice for many years, but decided to focus on working with children. My parents had set the date for his new specialization: January 1, 1930. Mother, always a skilled and careful investor, had been setting aside funds to see them through the expected lean years of the professional transition. Well, the big crash of October 1929 took place, and the bottom dropped out of their investments – but they decided to risk it anyway. It was during those days that Mother began to serve as Dad's office assistant – a job which they had expected to be temporary, but in which she continued until his retirement at age 80.

Our Weeks Avenue apartment was the ground floor of a two story, two family house, the center of a row of five such houses which shared a concrete back yard. We moved there when I was six and ready for first grade. We were across the street from P.S. 70, the first school which I remember attending, and to which I went until seventh grade, when Wade Junior High, P. S. 117, was built. I'm told that I had attended a Jewish kindergarten, as did my brother. Living across from school had distinct advantages. It was a quick trip home for lunch; I could get to music lessons and other after-school activities without delay; friends could visit on their way home from school, and, best of all, I was able to have my harp carried across the street for orchestra rehearsals. (A couple of the big eighth grade boys would carry it across and back – often grumbling that I should have taken up the piccolo.)

Mr. Tuttleman was our orchestra conductor, and he was very good to me. I suppose he was delighted to have a harp in his orchestra – certainly most public elementary schools could not say the same – and he adapted piano parts for me to use. Along with my harp teacher, Miss Nancy Morgan, he really helped me feel like a capable and valued musician. This was especially important to me as both my brother, Barry, and later my younger sister, Myra, turned out to have far more musical talent than did I. Additionally my father, a fine singer, would become impatient and irritable with me when, attempting to join the family harmony, I hit a wrong note. His periodic comment, "If you can't do it right, keep your mouth shut", rankles even in retrospect.

CHAPTER II: AND THEN WE WERE THREE

While living on Weeks Avenue, when I was seven and a half, my sister Isa Myra was born. I was thrilled beyond measure, and welcomed her with her own poem. It went like this:

Two blue eyes, a saucy nose;
Velvet cheeks, just like a rose.

Tiny hands with fingers long;
A voice that coos, just like a song.

Sweet sister mine, I'm glad you're here,
And I'll love you forever, dear.

Her crib was later put in my room, and I remember reciting and singing her to sleep. Barry and I were both very protective of her, and she grew up with what must have seemed to her as a double set of parents. She undoubtedly suffered from the stress of following two older siblings. The age difference meant that our minor setbacks or difficulties were forgotten, and just the aura of general success remained. I think she struggled all her life to catch up.

With three children, our home was becoming crowded, and when I was twelve we moved to 1840 Grand Concourse, on the fourth floor of the apartment building in which my father had his ground-floor office. This was in 1938, when landlords had many empty apartments, and perhaps a third of New York City moved on October 1st to take advantage of the free month's rent which was offered as an inducement. We were able to have two apartments put together, a five room with two bedrooms, and a two room next door. They had a wall in common, through which an arch was cut. The huge living room of the smaller apartment became Barry's bedroom, with the Murphy bed removed to make space for a closet. The kitchen was cleared of its fixtures to make a bedroom for Myra, while I had my bedroom in what had been the larger apartment. Of course, this arrangement also meant that we had two bathrooms – a genuine delight, until Barry converted one to serve as his darkroom when he went through his photographic period. We retained this double apartment partway into World War II; Barry was off in the Army and would be leaving for college when he returned; I was away at college, and apartments were very scarce in the city. Still, it felt weird to have strangers living in what had previously been part of our home.

The Bronx of my childhood was a very different place from what it is today. My father's family had been moving up in the world when they moved from the lower East Side of my father's birth to the more middle-class Bronx. Grand Concourse was the showplace of the West Bronx – a broad avenue with two tree-planted islands dividing the impressive six lanes of traffic. The side streets, however, continued to support some of the old immigrant ways. I remember the cry, "I cash clothes" of the ragman, the rattling bells of the knife and scissor grinder, and the clomp, clomp of horses' hooves as they traveled the streets pulling the open garbage or ice wagons. With so many horses around, we watched where we put our feet when crossing the street.

Though we had a refrigerator, many families still used iceboxes. They would put signs in their windows inscribed with large numbers - 25 or 50 - to indicate the number of pounds of ice that they wanted. Then the iceman would use his giant tongs to pick up the chunk of ice, put it over his shoulder, and trudge up two or three flights of stairs to where it was to be delivered. While he was gone, we children would climb on the back of the wagon to get ice chips on which to suck.

Of course, then as now, summer brought the ubiquitous tinkle of the ice cream truck. My father's strict rules forbade ice cream between meals, but we could tuck a pop into the ice cube section of the frig for later, unless we were lucky enough to be buying it right after lunch.

We were just a bus ride away from both the Bronx Botanical Gardens and the Bronx Zoo, each one an outstanding example of a public space. The Zoo, of course, was always filled with children, but the Garden presented a relatively quiet and peaceful atmosphere. During the polio epidemic of the late 1920's, Mother used to take Barry and me to the Botanical Gardens, where she would spread out a blanket, and play or read to us there. The idea was to keep us away from the risk of contagion presented by other children. She would take us rowing on the lake there, and later Barry and I did the rowing.

CHAPTER III: MY FAMILY

Dad was the oldest of four siblings – survivors of the seven children whom my grandmother had borne. Being both the oldest and male, as well as having been born in America, he had a great deal of authority in his immigrant family. His father had come to this country from Lithuania circa 1892. My grandmother was to follow as soon as her baby was born. Unfortunately, the baby died at birth, so Bubby came alone. Records were lost or destroyed in a fire, so Bubby did not have her ketubah, or marriage license, to prove that she was married to this young man who came to pick her up. As I was told the story; "they" would not let her go with him, so my grandparents were married again at Ellis Island. I wish I had thought to ask who "they" were; would the government have set such standards? I imagine it may have been HIAS, the Hebrew Immigrant Aid Society, whose members routinely met boats to save young girls from being tricked into prostitution.

The other thing I remember of that story was that Bubby, a religious orthodox Jewish woman to the end of her life, nonetheless took off her shaytle, the wig which religious married women were expected to wear, and declared, "I don't need to wear this any more; I'm in America now"! So perhaps I come by my feminism from both sides of the family.

It is of interest that I used Bubby's wedding ring, the same one which had served her at two weddings, at my own marriage. It fit beautifully. Now, with my fingers distorted by arthritis, I have had the ring incorporated with my engagement-ring diamond into a pendant which I wear around my neck at all times.

Mother's story had many parallels to Dad's. Her father had also left a pregnant wife, this one in the Ukraine, to follow him when the baby was born. This time it was the wife who died, and Mother stayed with various aunts and grandmothers until she was seven and a half, at which time her father remarried and sent for her. She traveled with an acquaintance of the family, to live with a father she had never met and a pregnant stepmother who didn't want her. School was her salvation, and the place where she came into her own. She not only became an avid reader, but preferring school to home, she attended even when she was sick, choosing to lie down in the nurse's office rather than remain at home with her stepmother. At her elementary school graduation she received a medal for never having missed a single day of school.

She also received a medal which was specially struck for her, indicating that she had received the highest mark in the history of admissions examinations for Hunter High School. (She earned perfect scores in every subject but English, where she was graded 99.7% on the theory that nobody could write a perfect essay!) My brother and I teethed on that medal.

By the time my sister came along, the medal had been stolen in a day-time break-in. I was six or seven at the time, and had something under a dollar in my allowance purse, money which the robber also took. The insurance adjuster sat down with me to discuss my loss. I was unsure of the exact amount, so he gravely handed me $1.50, to make sure that my loss was fully covered. But I was still quite uneasy. The robber had dropped one of our spoons as he carried away our flatware, and I feared he would come back to get it, so as to complete the set!

Alas, Mother was not to attend Hunter High. Her stepmother cried, "High school? What does a girl need with high school?

You'll go to work!" So Mother sadly got a job at Hearn's department store, as a cash girl, or 'runner', at $3.50 per week. From this munificent sum she paid her stepmother $2.50 a week – and never knew if her father was aware of this. But a few months into that job, she discovered that there was such a thing as evening high school. She enrolled the following fall, did four years of high school in three years at night, and was already at Hunter College when her elementary school classmates arrived.

Mother could never say enough good things about her teachers! Knowing their students all worked, these women came early and stayed late, to give them extra instruction time. One of her teachers took the same subway home as did Mother, and in their half-hour together gave her the equivalent of an extra year's work in Math. One, in fact, who had a sister teaching at Vassar, wanted Mother to apply there. She would provide the thousand dollars for the first year's tuition, and she was sure Mother could get a scholarship for the remainder. When Mother demurred at accepting such a gift, the teacher suggested they make it a loan. But Mother did not want to go into debt and chose to continue her plan to attend Hunter.

She loved Hunter; she became editor-in-chief of the Bulletin, introduced "Sing" to the college (for forty years her class gave the baton to the class which won that annual sing-off) and remained president of her class until her death at age 89. She continued to work for the Alumni Association throughout her life, and was inducted into the Hunter College Hall of Fame when in her eighties. When the city colleges began to charge a fee for students to attend, she and some classmates created the Hunter College Scholarship and Welfare fund, knowing that, had there been a charge earlier, she would have been unable to attend. A math major at college, she served the fund as treasurer for forty years, managing what became a two million dollar investment portfolio, until her resignation at age eight-two.

When Mother was sixty-five, I dreamed up what turned out to be the best birthday present she could have received. She hated receiving gifts, but I started a named scholarship for her in that very same fund – the Rose S. Golomb Scholarship Fund. I wrote to all her friends and our far-flung family members, and contributions to the fund poured in. Everybody who had contributed – over forty people – was invited to what Mother thought was a birthday party for Sherry. We put on a little skit, playing the parts of the admissions officer and the new applicant who needed financial help. Then a check was turned over to her – I believe it was for $2,700, a huge sum at that time. I had decorated a rectangular cake in the form of a check, made out to her scholarship fund and showing the total amount raised. Nothing could have thrilled Mother more. It was always difficult to decide what to give her on various occasions; now we could delight her while saving ourselves from that difficult decision-making, by contributing to her fund. Of course, as soon as it was listed in her college newsletters, classmates and other alumnae began to contribute, so the fund continued to grow. Thirty years later, inspired by that story, my children did the same for me – so there is a Sarai G. Zitter scholarship at the Wellesley Student Aid Society, to which family members often contribute on gift-giving occasions.

Dad's family, unlike Mother's, was immensely supportive of him in every way. He was very much the star, and the whole family worked together to send him to medical school. Even his younger siblings worked after school to help out. He took the subway to Queens six days a week; he started out the week with sixty-five cents in cash, ten cents daily for his carfare and a whole nickel to blow on whatever he liked!

To get a sense of what money was worth then: when I was engaged, we discovered that Sam and my father had grown up in the same part of the lower East Side, though obviously a generation apart. They had many similar experiences, such as sliding down a snowy hill on a garbage-can cover. Sam told of going to the movies for a nickel. Dad said, "A whole nickel? When I was a kid, we went in two-for-a-nickel. So if you had two cents, you'd hang around waiting for some rich kid with three cents, and you'd go in together!" That phrase "some rich kid with three cents" has always stayed with me, reminding me of my own good fortune.

But location mattered too. While Sam's movie cost a nickel, I, living in a better neighborhood, was paying ten cents and a penny tax for my local movie – if I went in before 1 PM. After that, the children's rate was twenty-five cents and a penny tax. As my whole allowance was only a quarter a week at that time, I made sure to be there before 1.

We also had a Matron in each theatre. There was a children's section, roped off for those under twelve, and the Matron saw to it that we were not molested or harassed by adult members of the audience. There were times in my early teens when I wished I still had that protection.

Dad and Mother made an interesting pair. Each had a strong personality and a clear sense of values. But they were very different indeed. Dad was quick-tempered, authoritative, insistent that his way was the right way. He was also handsome, charming and charismatic; people were drawn to him, and he had many friends. He was loving and protective, but demanding and sometimes unpredictable. He would blow up, lose his temper and yell, but never stayed angry for long. Five minutes later he wondered why you were angry with him. It amazed me that his patients adored him so, as he was as sharp and critical with them as he was with me. Yet I have heard him be gentle and considerate with a mentally limited parent. He had gone into medicine to help the poor and often saw indigent patients without charge. Yet for all the admiration I had for him, I found him difficult to deal with, and in our encounters I frequently emerged with hurt feelings. Dad had an excellent sense of humor – but there, too, he seemed unaware that people suffered when they were the butt of his jokes.

Mother was quite different. She was calm, supportive, reassuring – never lost her temper. There was never any doubt that she was in charge, but I never felt she bossed me around. While she articulated her wishes and her priorities, she was also a good listener. And her sense of integrity was absolute. I remember our saying that, if her body were to collapse, her integrity would hold her up! Significantly, she was not a worrier, and I can give that fact much credit that I, too, have been spared much of that distressing emotion. She was immensely practical; I do not think there were many things to which she could not turn her hand. She fixed electric wires, did carpentry and minor household repairs, reupholstered furniture – in short, did whatever needed to be done. From making clothes to making pies, she found ways to learn what she felt she needed to know. It was she to whom we went for anything that needed doing – with the exception of a doll or teddy bear in need of healing. Those we took to Dad for one of his famous bandages! He also painted smiling mercurochrome faces on skinned knees, and carved a terrific jack-o-lantern!

Both of them were also active in the community – Dad in Jewish affairs as well as medical matters, and Mother with things like the League of Women Voters (of which she was a founding member), the Girl Scouts, and her beloved Hunter College. They were also central in our extended family. As I grew up, I learned that everyone saw my parents as exceptional

– and I was both proud of them, and intimidated by the thought that I could never achieve what they had done.

As one might expect, we were much closer to Dad's family than to Mother's. The Golombs also had the advantage of location – like us, they lived in the Bronx, while Mother's family was way out in Brooklyn. The Golombs were a close-knit clan; the siblings maintained a closeness and affection which lasted throughout their lives and set the stage for the close cousin relationships which I enjoy. Mollie was three years Dad's junior; then came Sambo (really Joel, but that sounded so much like Joe that they switched to his middle name, Simon, which then became Sambo!) and last was the baby, Shulamuth, called Shully by us all. We got together on Friday nights and all the Jewish holidays, first at Bubby's and later at my parents' home. Though the Friday nights disappeared as the families grew, the holidays continued as extended family gatherings throughout their lives and mine. Eventually the milieu shifted to my home, later alternated with that of my cousins Judi and Lee. And while the family eventually became so large and so scattered that we could not spend all the holidays together, we continue to this day the tradition of having extended family gatherings at least a couple of times a year.

When I speak of family, I must include Aunt Sophie and Uncle Lou Nadler. They were close friends of my parents, and though not blood-relations, I cannot think of my childhood without them. They had no children of their own, though Aunt Sophie had suffered several miscarriages. Her one live child, born at around the same time as I, died within an hour of birth. I have always suspected that this made me especially dear to them. Aunt Sophie was a gentle, quiet woman, barely five feet tall but large of heart, always loving and supportive. When I was little and decided to run away from home, it was to Aunt

Sophie that I went. (She assured me that she would love to have me, but reminded me that, with her poor eyesight, she would not be able to read to me. I decided to stay home!) Uncle Lou, tall and jovial, was a kidder and joker par excellence. He clearly adored children, and it was always fun being with Uncle Lou. I might mention that my children enjoyed the same loving relationship with the Nadlers as had I.

When I first became aware of the possibility of parents dying, I began to think about with whom I would live. I visualized all my aunts and uncles vying for the privilege of having me. Aunt Shully, Aunt Mollie, Aunt Sophie – none had any children at that time, and I just knew they would all want me. Whom would I select? It never occurred to me that the choice would not be mine. Fortunately, that was one decision with which I never had to cope.

As I've mentioned, we were a singing family, and our gatherings always included music. They also included lots of food, and I began cooking and baking at a very early age. We often had twenty to twenty-five people around the table for various holidays. Mother was wonderfully patient as a teacher, and she always made sure that I got full credit for my part in the preparations. I always assumed that Mother loved to cook, and in my identification with her I also loved it. Many years later I discovered that she never enjoyed it much; she did such a lot because it was needed, not for pleasure. But by then I was already hooked! (The same thing happened with sewing. During the Depression Mother made many of my clothes. I loved learning to sew, and only as an adult found that this had not been a joy for Mother, as I had thought, but something she did cheerfully because it was a way to save money.)

As in every Jewish family, Passover was a major event each year. It was our custom to sing between courses at dinner, as well as the singing involved in reading the service. Our dining-room windows faced a concrete yard, as did those of many of our neighbors. One year it was quite cool at Passover time, and our windows were closed. Part-way through the service came a timid knock on the door. It was our neighbor, asking if we could please open our windows; they were having trouble hearing the singing!

I was twelve when we moved to the Concourse, and some member of our family continued to live there until my sister's untimely death at age sixty-three. Junior high school was a new concept at that time, taking as it did two years from the end of elementary school plus the first year of high school. A junior high opened in my neighborhood when I was in seventh grade, and the students from P.S. 70 carried our own books, walking the several blocks which separated the two schools. I spent only a year and a half there, as the high school which I chose to attend, Music and Art, preferred to have its students for the full four years. Thus I was deprived of a graduation ceremony in both elementary school and junior high. I always enjoyed school, and learning came easily to me. The only subjects which gave me trouble (before college!) were geography and foreign languages. I excelled at English and got much encouragement for my creative writing. However, I lacked the drive which might have made me an outstanding student, and was quite satisfied with my grades in the mid to high eighties.

CHAPTER IV: MY ACTIVE LIFE

An important element in my life was the Girl Scouts. Mother, who had been a founding member of the Bronx Girl Scout Council, was our troop leader. Her pre-marital years as a hiker and mountain climber stood us in good stead, as she gave us city-bred girls a wonderful taste of the outdoors. We went on frequent hikes to the Palisades, just over the Hudson River in New Jersey. Earlier, she had taken Barry and me not only on hikes, but on overnight camping trips there as well. Along with Girl Scout camp in the summer, those were among my happiest days. The ethic of Girl Scouting resonated with me; I found - and still find – a deep emotional response to the ideals of friendship and community responsibility which the scout laws embody.

There is something in me which resonates at being part of something much larger than myself. I feel it as a Jew, reciting prayers that have belonged to my heritage for thousands of years, and knowing that Jews all over the world are reciting the same prayers to commemorate the same holidays. I feel it as an American, pledging to honor and support my country, and believing that one of my highest responsibilities is to work to set and keep her on the proper track towards our highest democratic ideals. And yes, I feel it as a Girl Scout, no longer active in Scouting but still committed to a movement which reaches women and girls around the world.

Soon after I joined the Girl Scouts, Schrafts ran a baking contest for the Girl Scouts of Greater New York. An experienced baker, I entered a loaf cake, iced in light green and sporting the Girl Scout Trefoil in a darker green frosting. I wrote about that event in a recent issue of my community news magazine, The Cabot Chronicle. Here it is.

CAN SHE BAKE A CHERRY PIE ?

At age ten and a newly-minted Girl Scout, I was delighted to learn that Schrafts, the mammoth ice cream salon and candy and cookie manufacturer, was sponsoring a baking contest for the Girl Scouts of New York City. I had been baking since I was six; this was a natural for me.

My light-as-a feather loaf cake was iced in pale green and decorated with the Girl Scout trefoil in a darker shade of green. I placed second in the Bronx but failed to place in the final five-borough run-off. Well, it was a good start, and I determined that I would do better the following year. What I did not know was that the previous year had featured cookies, leaving the year ahead as an unknown.

A month before the contest date, it was announced: we were to bake a cherry pie. I was devastated – I had never baked a pie in my life. I went to my mother with my tale of woe. Ever practical, she shrugged; didn't I have a whole month in which to learn?

So, highly organized, we set to work. Every day after school, I baked a pie. I tried pie crust with Crisco, with butter, with oil. I tried the light Queen Anne cherries, dark and sweet cherries, and everything in between. (That was before the days of frozen fruit, or we would have tried that, too.) I thickened with corn starch; I thickened with flour; I thickened with tapioca. I tried fillings both cooked and uncooked. I experimented with cloth versus a board for rolling. I learned how to add additional shortening, fold and re-roll, for extra flakiness. I learned to roll from the middle out, rather than forward and back, to maintain an even thickness in the crust. I learned how to keep the bottom crust from becoming soggy – brush it with egg-white before adding the filling – and how to give the top crust or lattice a pleasing light brown – brush it with beaten egg yolk slightly thinned with water. Naturally, I kept records and charts detailing my results.

But the great day came, and it was all worthwhile! I placed first in the Bronx and second in the city, and was rewarded with a huge basket of Schraft goodies.

Several years later, during World War II, my high school was raising money to buy an ambulance for the Red Cross. My contribution was to take cake-baking orders from teachers, with the profit going to the ambulance fund. I got many kudos for my baking, but never did they rival the satisfaction of that giant basket from Schrafts and the knowledge that, in a single month, I had become a prize-winning baker of pies!

I should mention that my brother never cared for cherry pie, so every now and then I provided an apple pie, especially for him.

Two or three years later, the Girl Scouts gave me another baking opportunity. The Bronx Girl Scout Council was celebrating its 10th birthday – an affair planned for scout leaders, with Lou Henry Hoover, wife of the former president, as guest speaker. Mrs. Hoover was at that time national honorary president of the Girl Scouts of America. I baked a birthday cake for the occasion and wrote a poem to go with it. I was thrilled to receive a note of appreciation from Mrs. Hoover, in her own handwriting, thanking me for my contribution and saying how impressed she was with my skill both with flour and with words.

Someone once asked my daughter Sherry when she had first become a feminist. She said that it was about sixty years before she was born, when her grandmother marched for women's suffrage. I also was born a feminist. I could always accept that my brother had a privilege denied me because he was two years older than I, but never could I tolerate a distinction based on gender. In those days gender discrimination was the norm, but in my family most of the expectations and opportunities were more egalitarian. I give my mother major credit for this, as she was the one who spent most time with us. Under her tutelage we all learned to cook and sew as well as to paint and do simple carpentry. She strongly believed that everybody must learn to take care of him- or herself; wealth could be lost and spouses could die, but your skills would always remain yours. Clearly her own life experiences had helped to develop this philosophy, and we were very much its beneficiaries. The greatest advantage of this to me was that I never felt the pressure to get married which so many young women experienced. My mother's attitude was: the only reason to get married is if you love someone so much that you can't imagine life without him; otherwise, you're better off single! And by empowering her daughters to be independent, she made it clear that no one should need to marry just to be taken care of.

An early example of my feminism was at Simchas Torah the year I was six. My brother, age eight, was carrying a small Torah in the celebratory parade that marked the end and beginning of the annual reading of the Torah. With satisfaction, I declared, "And in two years I'll be able to carry that!" Our elderly rabbi smiled benignly. "Nein, Tochter", he said – i.e., "no, daughter; carrying the torah is only for boys." As Mother described it, I flew at him like a ptarmigan; "But girls are supposed to be good Jews, and..and..girls are supposed to keep Kosher homes, and..and...girls are supposed to go to shul...But they can't carry the Torah? That's not fair!" According to Mother, the poor rabbi never knew what hit him.

Yet that sense of unfairness always troubled me in relation to Orthodox Judaism. I felt strongly that women were treated unequally in the religious sphere, and never felt totally at home in my religion until I found Reform Judaism, with its more egalitarian, gender-neutral approach.

CHAPTER V: SCHOOL DAYS

In those days, although there was no school uniform as such, we were expected to wear a specific outfit for Assembly – for boys, a white shirt and dark pants, and for the girls, a white middy-blouse and dark skirt, with a red scarf knotted at the neck. Many the day that I came home with blue streaks down the back of my blouse; the boy sitting behind me could never resist dipping my braids into the inkwell.

What, you may wonder, was an inkwell? Well, in each desk we had a small hole in the upper right-hand corner which held an open cup. In this we mixed dry ink powder with water. Then, after inserting the metal nib, or pen point, into the holder – a long stick, thicker at the bottom, with a crescent line slit into it to hold the nib – we would dip the pen into the inkwell, shake off the excess ink, and write. Usually we could get several words written for each dip of the pen; sometimes the writing was so wet that we needed to use a blotter. (A blotter is a porous paper which absorbed excess liquid – an essential when using this kind of ink.) It would have been simpler to use a fountain pen – but that was for adults. I received my first fountain pen when I finished elementary school. One still, however, needed ink with which to fill it. Such a pen was considered so special that it was frequently used as a Bar Mitzvah gift, giving rise to the old joke about the Bar Mitzvah boy who, intending to start his speech with "Today I am a man!" said instead, "Today I am a fountain pen!" Our modern ballpoint pens had yet to be invented.

Though I stammered somewhat in ordinary talking, I was quite good, even dramatic, with prepared material, whether memorized or read aloud. More than once I introduced a class play or activity at assembly, or read the chosen bible portion. (Yes, assemblies in those days – at least in my school - started with the reading of a selection from the bible.) This was from a very early age; when in second grade I offered the following original presentation:

Good morning, friends; class 2A1
Welcomes you today.
We hope you will enjoy our fun,
Our music, and our play.

We've had a very lovely time
Preparing you this play,
And if you show you like it,
We'll all be very gay.

I still recall an assembly poem that I wrote for our semi-annual school magazine:

Oh, let me tell you, Mother dear,
Today we have Assembly,
And I must wear my nice blue skirt,
Red tie, and whitest middy;

And I must make my shoes to shine,
For that is most important,
And we shall have the straightest line
And 'perfect' in deportment.

My elementary school was divided into lower, kindergarten through 4th grade, and upper, 5th through 8th grades. The overall principal was Mr. Schoenberg, and he handled the upper grades. Mrs. Berg, the Assistant Principal, was responsible for the lower grades. She was very fond of me and encouraged my writing for the school magazine from first grade on.

Once, when I was in fourth grade, she met me in the hall and mentioned how disappointed she was that I had not submitted a poem for the next issue of the magazine. So I told her my story.

I had turned in a poem to my teacher, Mrs. Wanamaker. It went more or less like this (I think I have forgotten a verse or two):

> I love to study geography
> And learn of children over the sea,
>
> What they do and what they wear
> And if their skin is dark or fair;
>
> How they live, and what they eat,
> And if their homes are clean and neat.
>
> For Mother says – and I know it's true -
> The difference is in what they do;
>
> What they are is like you and me,
> These little children over the sea.

Not too shabby for a fourth grader. But Mrs. Wanamaker felt that the rhythm was off; she wanted me to change "over" in the first and last verses to "o'er". I objected, saying that I never used words in my verses which I didn't use in general speech. She insisted she would change it, and I refused to allow it to appear over my name if it wasn't entirely mine. We were at an impasse, and the poem was not sent it. Mrs. Berg heard me out, said she was sorry to have missed my poem, and hoped I would submit both it and a new one for the next issue; both would be printed!

As I have mentioned, New York City schools operated in half year units, and 'skipping' a term was not uncommon. By dint of this, I was only twelve and a half when it was time to think of high school. I am always amused when I hear talk of "Magnet Schools" as if they were something new; we had them in New York as early as the nineteen thirties. Our forward-looking mayor, Fiorello H. LaGuardia, had initiated several of them. Unlike most public high schools, they required testing for admission, so they offered an excellent academic atmosphere as well as specialized education in a particular area. One, the Bronx High School of Science, had attracted my brother. It was less than a mile from home, and he usually walked to and from school. I, however, was interested in the High School of Music and Art, located at 135th street and Convent Avenue, at the upper edge of Harlem. The music testing was more for musical potential than actual performance, and I was thrilled to be admitted. Attendance required a subway ride, followed by a ten minute walk through a park and up a steep flight of stairs. It took me about thirty-five minutes all told, but we had students who traveled almost two hours, from the other end of Brooklyn, for the privilege of attending this incredible school. I thought about that in the sixties, when I heard arguments over the bussing of children to help remedy racial imbalance in the schools. I also wished that my own children could have had access to a school like Music and Art.

Music and Art was an amazing experience. Unlike at many high schools, everyone was there by choice, so a sense of purpose, even dedication, pervaded the place. In addition to the usual six periods of academic subjects, we had three periods of music or art daily, so the day was a long one. Yet after-school musical jamming sessions were common, and ad hoc musical combos sprang up frequently. Art students had to take music appreciation and music students the reverse. I must admit that art never gripped me, and I think I have something akin to the artistic equivalent of tone-deafness. But music has continued to play an important role throughout my life.

M&A had six orchestras, and usually one worked one's way up through the ranks. As a further benefit of playing the harp, however, I was put immediately into the senior orchestra, a much-coveted opportunity. Not only was it of really professional quality, with members who went on to become significant figures in the musical world, but we also had guest conductors of amazing ability. Leonard Bernstein, then a young conductor on his way up, conducted us on more than one occasion, and I remember a Negro conductor, Dean Dixon, whom we all thought was at least as good.

When high school started, we were asked to choose someone with whom to share a locker. A girl who had played violin in my elementary school orchestra suggested we share a locker – and thus began a lifelong friendship. Ellie lived a few blocks from me and got on the subway one station down from mine. We usually traveled to and from school together and spent much of our spare time in each other's company. When we spent time together on a Friday or Saturday evening, we planned to walk one another to a point midway between our homes and then separate. However, we would get to talking, not notice where we were, and find ourselves way past that spot. So we would walk back – and often do the same thing again. Many times we gave up, walked to her house to leave a note for her mother, and then walked back to my house for an impromptu sleep-over. In the morning, when Mother knocked at my door, she would look into my room and see twins!

The reason we slept at my house is that I had my own room. Ellie's family was very poor and lived in a tiny, crowded apartment, where she shared a bedroom with her sister. I did not realize until much later that her family had been living on the edge of poverty during those years. I recall that I once asked my mother for advice on what to buy Ellie for her birthday, and Mother suggested a blouse or a slip. I declared that clothing was not a real gift. Mother, with a very different life experience from mine, responded, "It is if you don't have enough!" I had never noticed that my friend's wardrobe was limited almost to the point of shabbiness!

I entered high school in February of 1940. I have no idea whether playing the harp was a factor in my admission, but I loved high school from day one. I was never part of a 'crowd', but always had one or two close friends, and that seemed sufficient.

CHAPTER VI: THE WAR YEARS

On December 7, 1941, in what President Roosevelt called "a day that will live in infamy", we were attacked by the Japanese at Pearl Harbor and thus drawn into World War II. The war was a backdrop to everything in our lives for the next four years. I was fifteen and a high school sophomore, but my seventeen year old brother wanted to enlist immediately. He was graduating from high school, and my parents convinced him to begin college so that he would have a place to come back to after the war. They promised then to sign his enlistment papers.

Everything was condensed in time. Colleges were running summer terms in order to move students – male students, that is – along quickly, so they could enlist. ROTC units popped up in all the colleges. Barry went off to Harvard as planned, but it was clear from his grades that his heart was not in it. The only A he received that first year was in ROTC. I think that Dad allowed him to go out of town to college, because it gave him more bargaining power to keep Barry from immediate enlistment. And when my turn came, I think Barry having gone out-of-town may have been a factor in helping along my own out-of-town college plans.

I vividly recall the night of Barry's graduation. He was due at Harvard on Saturday, the last day for registration, and his graduation was Friday night. The whole family attended, with Barry's bags packed and waiting in Dad's car. Then they stopped at home, left me to baby-sit 7 year old Myra, and drove Barry to Grand Central Station to catch the midnight train to Boston. I was devastated at not being able to see him off, but nonetheless took my baby-sitting responsibilities quite seriously. Although at some level I knew better, I think I half-believed that Myra had been born in response to my persistent pleas for a baby sister.

On the home front, we were all committed to doing our part for the war effort. We bought war bonds, saved aluminum foil and rubber bands, and contributed to the Red Cross and the USO. We even had to turn in old toothpaste tubes in order to be able to buy a new one - the metal in the tubes was being re-used. Certain foods were scarce, and we shopped with ration cards. We never faced the food shortages that Europe had to deal with, but many small luxuries were no longer available. Sugar and butter were scarce, and that is when margarine (called oleomargarine) first came on the market. It was sold in white quarter-pound or pound sticks, with a little capsule of yellow coloring which we could blend into it to make it resemble butter. Without that, it looked like Crisco. Of course, as it was totally vegetable in origin, kosher homes could for the first time serve a butter-like spread with meat meals. However, if it looked too much like butter, many older Orthodox Jews still could not face it at their tables when meat was being served.

A few years later, rationing gave me the topic for a verse which we were assigned to write in one of my college English classes:

> Time was when I was free from woe;
> I looked on no man as a foe.
> My door to all was open wide,
> For naught worth stealing lay inside.
>
> A fortress now my home must be,
> Guarded 'neath fool-proof lock and key,
> And every window I'll secure

With iron bars to long endure.

I have no gold or silver bright,
No emeralds, pearls for which to fight,
And treasures rare I do not own,
Nor silks, nor lace, nor precious stone.

But I've one thing I cannot spare –
The only thing I will not share;
I'll keep it safe by hook or crook –
My love! My life! My ration book!

My high school decided to buy an ambulance to give to the Red Cross. All kinds of fund-raising were instituted, and many of us found individual ways of raising money. One of our art students made linoleum block carvings from which to stamp out book plates; for my five dollars – which went, not to the student, but to the Ambulance Fund – I got a book plate stamp with a harp, a music stand, and a book carved on it. I decided to use my baking skills; I recently came across a copy of the note which I had put in teachers' boxes at school. It reads like this:

DO YOU LIKE HOME-BAKED CAKES?
DO YOU WANT TO SWELL OUR AMBULANCE FUND
IS THE ANSWER TO BOTH QUESTIONS "YES"?
Read on....

I, Sarai Golomb, being of sound mind (?), have decided that my one sure way of making money to add to our ambulance fund lies in my baking ability. For the next number of weeks, therefore, I should like to receive orders for cakes to be brought to school on Mondays or on schooldays following a holiday.

MOTHER will supply the ingredients.
I will supply the time and labor.
YOU will supply the cash.
THE AMBULANCE FUND will reap the benefit.

Women Teachers: Why worry about dessert on Monday night? Let me do it for you.
Men Teachers: Give the little woman a break! Nobody likes to eat her own baking all the time.
Unmarried Teachers: You can eat it all yourself.

Plain Cake   Apple Sauce Cake   Devil's Food   Gingerbread

Price: sixty cents per cake Vegetable shortening used

Sarai Golomb 6-1

I don't remember specifics, but I know I did a brisk business with my Sunday baking. It felt good to be able to make my own special contribution to this vital fund. My brother was overseas at the time, and this gave an extra spur to my dedication. Reference was made to this effort when class notes were written for our senior yearbook. Under my picture appeared:

She's the harpist of the class,
This smiling, patriotic lass.

Many of the activities which I had earlier done with my mother and brother, I now enjoyed with my friends – roller skating and ice-skating, bike riding and swimming. I never was a sun lover – in fact, I avoided it when possible – but did enjoy the outdoors in general, swimming and hiking in particular. I often used my bike for transportation; the city was a safer place for biking then than it is now. Interestingly, a friend of mine recently reminded me that when I was working at a social agency at 149th Street in the Bronx, I sometimes biked to work. In my teens I joined the American Youth Hostels and spent many happy weekends or Sundays hiking, biking or camping overnight with that dedicated outdoor group. We often took our bikes on the subway to our meeting place, but on occasion I rode from my home on 176th Street all the way down to AYH headquarters at 34th Street, a feat I would not wish to attempt in today's traffic. I still have my lifetime membership card in AYH, and am delighted to see bike lanes now being established in many parts of New York City.

I cannot leave my childhood days without speaking of my Girl Scout camp, Laughing Water. (My brother irreverently called it Ha-Ha-Trickle-Trickle – but he loved the Boy Scout camp he attended as much as I did mine!) The sessions were two weeks each, at $10 a week. I was incredibly lucky; my parents were able to afford a full month each summer, at a grand total of $40. I went every summer until I was past fifteen and almost ready for college. Many of the songs I learned there are with me to this day. My camping days, along with the experiences I had with my mother and brother in the Palisades, started me on a lifelong love of hiking, camping and all sorts of outdoor skills. In later years, as a Girl Scout leader in New Jersey, I had a hiking-oriented troop of my own, and taught outdoor skills – maps, compass, fire-building, etc. – to other scout leaders in my town. Although my husband's recollections of camping entailed sleeping in the mud in China during the war – a very different nostalgia from my own - I was able to persuade him to try camping, and this proved to be our family's preferred mode of vacation for many years. We graduated from a borrowed tent to a large tent of our own to a pop-up tent-trailer. Again, it is a pleasure to see my own children, especially my daughters, continue to enjoy hiking and camping throughout their lives.

With my creative mother at the helm, our Girl Scout troop became involved in quite a number of interesting projects, many offering a community-service aspect. Although I loved all the activities, our hikes in the Palisades were a primary source of delight. I particularly recall a Sunrise Hike. Walking through dark and empty city streets, we met at the subway station at 174th Street at 4 A.M. and took the subway down to 145th Street. Here we transferred to the Washington Heights line and went uptown to 181st Street. After a walk of several blocks, we were at the George Washington Bridge and started across the span in the fading darkness. Just as we reached the center of the bridge, the sun crested the skyline behind us, and we were bathed in its brightness. It felt as if the sun had come out especially for us! To this day, I marvel that Mother was able to time it so well; never will I believe that the magical timing was purely accidental!

That bridge was quite new at the time. Its construction had been completed the summer before my sixth birthday, and I remember walking across it that first year with my mother and brother. (Dad, though quite athletic and a top-notch tennis player, was a dedicated non-walker!) Although we often took the ferry to New Jersey, the bridge gave us an easier and quicker connection. Most of my hikes and bike trips started and ended with that crossing.

After completing his first year of college in seven months, Barry enlisted in the Army. He got his basic training in Oklahoma, and during his time there we often sent him food packages, including home-baked cakes. We saved our sugar rations for this purpose. Though in the Infantry, when he was sent to Europe he became a forward observer for the Field

Artillery, moving ahead of the front lines to help direct their fire. It was probably one of the most dangerous of positions, but he liked it because he was depending on himself, rather than others, to look after him. I am glad we did not know about it until he came home.

My grandmother lived next door to us. Like us all, she was worried about Barry's safety. In those days, household mail was delivered twice a day, but business and professionals, like my father, got three deliveries daily. My grandmother would come in to ask about mail from Barry, and when we had a letter, would breathe, "Thank God! At least we know he's safe!" Mother realized more starkly, of course, that it only meant he had been safe two or three weeks earlier, when he had written the letter. Then Bubby would often reassure Mother that "Don't worry. God will take care of him." Mother sometimes could not help replying, "You mean He'll get some other mother's son killed instead of mine?" Bubby was shocked! "Oh, no. God will take care of all of them." But clearly, soldiers do die. Mother, a math major at college, knew that 90% of the boys were likely to come home; she preferred to put her faith in the law of averages.

How did I ever get to Wellesley? Dad didn't really approve of girls going away from home for college; he felt they should live with their parents until they got married. He used the pretext that they couldn't afford it, and said I could go if I could get a scholarship. I was a high average student, but certainly not at the top grade-wise; I'm sure he didn't believe I could get one. But I applied to Radcliff, Barnard and Wellesley, seeking a merit scholarship at each. I was admitted to Radcliff, but without a scholarship. Barnard wait-listed me, as they did with most New York applicants. But Wellesley not only admitted me, but gave me a small scholarship for the first year. It was enough; Dad had to give in.

Sarai G. Zitter

Why did they want a student who was not at the very top of her class? I have two suppositions on that score. First, I imagine that my playing the harp may have been a factor. But more important, I had superb recommendations from all my teachers. I had been active in all service groups at high school, contributed my services in many areas and to many teachers, did all the mimeographing for the math office, and in general was one of those people who could always be called on to lend a helping hand. But whatever the reason, that small scholarship – which was not renewed the following year – did the trick, and I was off to one of the major experiences of my life.

Many years later, I heard what news commentator Gabriel Heater would have called "the rest of the story." Mother had said to Dad, "You always want to give me something. You want to get me jewelry; I don't wear jewelry. You want to get me a fur coat; I don't want a fur coat. Here is something I want; give me Sis's college!" He couldn't say no.

This was 1943, and our national focus was all on the war effort. In my high school, there had been a contest for an original patriotic song, and it had been won, of all things, by an art student. Though I cannot recall his name, I still remember both words and melody:

There's a lady in the harbor,
She's been standing there for years,
And she's carrying the torch for you;
She's a symbol of the light
Of freedom burning bright,
She's a symbol of the job you have to do:

Come on, Yankee Doodle, let's win the war.
Get in there and fight like you did before.

Shoulder to shoulder, with flags unfurled.
You must go forward to free the world!

Come on, Yankee Doodle, and make them pay
For all that they did on Pearl Harbor Day.
The people are cheering and rooting for you!
Come on, Yankee Doodle, come through!

Although I had been somewhat successful when I wrote harp
music for our semi-annual Original Compositions Concert, my
own song offering did not do as well. It went like this:

Over there, over here, there's a job to be done
Everyone must be clear that we're coming on the run.
Now we're should'ring the ax 'gainst the Axis;
Soon we'll start making saps out of Japses;
And we'll make the world free
For democracy
In the good old American way.

Everyone must enroll, soldier, sailor and the rest;
Everyone must be told where his work fits in the best –
Whether dropping the bombs that will shatter,
Or buying War Bonds that will matter –
If it makes the world free,
It's democracy
In the good old American way.

When the fighting shall cease, a new order will begin.
When we've won a just peace, happy days we'll usher in.
Into plowshares our guns will be pounded;
Men will live by the freedoms we've founded;
And the whole world will be
A democracy
In the good old American way!

45

Looking back, I'm shocked by my use of the term 'Japses', but I wish nonetheless that my prediction had turned out to be true! That was the last war we have waged in which our entire country felt fully engaged, pulled together, and were by and large ready to offer shared sacrifice.

I was a little young for college. In addition to having skipped three semesters during elementary school (not too unusual for a bright New York City student at that time) I realized that I would complete high school in January – fine for a city college, which also ran on the semester system, but leaving me with several months to fill before starting college. So I went to summer school to garner the extra classes in Math and English which I would need in order to graduate a semester early, in June. Most of the summer students were there to make up for failed courses, so I was easily the star of each class. When I received my report card, I had quite a shock! The grade in Math was 95 - but in English, always my best subject, it was 65! I had never seen a 65 on a report card before. My ever-practical mother suggested that I go downtown that very day and talk with the teacher, before the summer school was closed. So I did, and found that the teacher had been delighted with my work – clearly top-drawer stuff - and didn't understand my consternation. Sixty-five was a passing grade, wasn't it? I asked if she felt that represented my work – and she asked if 75 would be better. I explained that the grade would be going on my college applications, which she clearly had never considered; for most of the summer students, passing was the only concern. Would I prefer 85? I think I could have talked her up to a 98, but we settled, if I recall, for 90.

Camp had been the focus of my previous summers, but I was ready for new challenges. A call was sent out for high school and college women from the city to join in a save-the-crop mission in upstate New York. The men who were the usual workers were mostly, of course, in the service. I responded with enthusiasm and found myself (accompanied by my friend Ellie who, like me, had also accelerated to graduate in June) in a camp near Red Hook, NY. Our chaperones were a professor from Cooper Union and his wife, and there were many Cooper students there as well. I became friendly with several of them, and met one, a woman two years my senior, who became one of my dearest life-long friends. Phyllis – we called her Flip – shared my love of music and poetry. We sang folk music together; she introduced me to Union songs; we discovered a mutual affection for Dorothy Parker, whose verse we often quoted to one another – and, sixty-seven years later, still do! We wrote songs about the woes of strawberry picking, and reveled in the happy coincidence that we both lived in the Bronx.

I might add that Flip was the first woman ever to graduate from Cooper Union as a Mechanical Engineer. Later, she was also the first woman in the United States to be appointed to a State Board for Engineering and Land Surveying. Yet when first looking for a job, she had great difficulties – because she was a woman! She did have some interesting engineering jobs during her career, however, and ultimately wound up teaching Engineering Technology at Bronx Community College for twenty years. It is her home in Schroon Lake that I have visited every summer for years, and her home in Florida where I often stay for a week in winter. Our friendship is one of those which have nurtured and sustained me through the years – and I know it has been the same for her.

We returned to farming camp the following summer. A few days into the session, the young man who served as our janitor was called up for service in the Navy. A new janitor was needed, and I stepped into the breach. I rose daily at 5 AM to shovel coal into the furnace, so that there would be hot water for our morning ablutions. I did occasional minor repairs, but mainly relaxed during much of the day, reactivating the furnace by mid-afternoon for the returning laborers' showers. Also, I chlorinated the swimming pool – achieved by swimming around towing a cheesecloth bag filled with powdered, gradually-dissolving chlorine.

CHAPTER VII: AT WELLESLEY

College was, in some ways, a mixed experience for me. I was really too young when I started - not yet seventeen – and quite unsophisticated. It was wartime, so men were scarce even in nearby colleges like Harvard and MIT. I loved the beautiful campus, the fine old ivy-covered buildings, and reveled in many of the traditions. I enjoyed the camaraderie of the other girls and found my classes to be challenging and exciting. As has always been typical of me, I got involved in many different activities, and my grades were poor that first year. It was partly my poor choice of courses: I had decided to get out of the way those courses which I thought I would not like – so my freshman classes included math and chemistry, as well as a medieval history course that somehow included maps and geography. I had thought I was good at math, but began to realize that much of my understanding of it had been due to my mother's help. And chemistry was very difficult; I never saw through the microscope what I was told to expect, and while it was fun pouring something into something else and seeing it turn blue, I never really got the hang of it. I remember my teacher, Miss Jones, saying to me, "You have an 'A' mind, Miss Golomb; why do you consistently do 'D' work in chemistry?" I could not find a way to explain that I had an 'A' mind in English, but not in chemistry.

Every year I made sure to give myself one 'dessert' course – something that would be sheer delight. That was usually English. By passing a test, I had been exempt from the usual freshman English, which I believe was mainly composition. I was also exempt from freshman Hygiene, which gave me a chance to take Miss Wells' course in English Folk Music. That was undiluted joy! My interest in folk music, both English and

American, has never abated, and in later years when I learned to play the guitar, folk music was always my métier.

I had started college planning to major in English, my ultimate goal being journalism. But as soon as I met my first psychology course, I was hooked! It was not so much that I loved it, but that somehow I recognized it. It felt right, and from then on I never considered another career. This was, of course, during the war, and many of us were knitting baby clothes for the Red Cross, or watch helmets for the Navy. We asked permission to knit in our psychology class, and a quite reasonable edict was handed down: if a student could maintain a B average, she would be permitted to knit – otherwise, not! I majored in Psychology and minored in Sociology, but if you were to include Latin and Greek Literature in translation, I had enough English credits for a major as well. I learned to do homework in my less-favorite subjects first, saving the English homework for dessert.

I might mention the one award I won while at college. The Junior Poetry Award was given each year to the junior who had the best poetry collection and wrote the best article describing how it was put together and what it meant to the student. My books were always the first thing I unpacked each year, and in my junior year I made sure to bring all my poetry volumes with me. I believe a faculty committee came to view my books. Though my essay has been lost and I now don't even recall what the prize was, I do know that it was exciting to win that award.

I played the harp in the orchestra my first year at college, but although it probably was fine for a college orchestra, I had been spoiled by the professionalism of the senior orchestra at Music and Art, and did not continue it at Wellesley. I was involved with theatre during my four years – mostly not, alas, on the stage, though I did have a small part in my Junior Show and played the lead in a Theatre Workshop production. I was on the food committee from the first, and served as its head during senior year. As the cast and crews could not get back to their dorms in time for dinner, we served up to thirty people at the theatre in Alumni Hall every night during dress-rehearsal week. Truthfully, I was the one who knew how to cook, and with my committee produced delicious meals, soup to dessert, for about thirty-five cents apiece. I learned to make boiled coffee – the grounds wrapped in a piece of cheesecloth and dropped into the huge coffee pot to boil – and to clarify the resulting coffee by dropping in a couple of eggshells at the end.

A favorite course was Theatre Workshop. Our final exam was to select, cast, costume and do makeup for a one-act play, which was then offered to the college community. As a freshman I had acted an old man in someone else's play, "The Rogue in the Bed," and when it came my turn I selected James M. Barrie's "The Twelve Pound Look." The theme is much like that of Ibsen's "The Doll House" and was well-suited to my ongoing feminist consciousness.

Another favorite activity was the weekly Step-singing. I don't believe I ever missed attending it and was an enthusiastic participant in some of the back-and-forth exchange of songs between the classes. In our senior year we often wore our academic gowns to step-singing; what a sight we must have been. Again, I am blessed with remembering the words to most of the songs, and I enjoy them still!

From the beginning I participated in IOCA, the Intercollegiate Outing Club Association. Included were students from Harvard, Radcliff, MIT, Boston College, U. Mass and many others in the area. Several groups went hiking on Sundays, sometimes skiing or rock-climbing, and occasionally spent a weekend camping. It was our custom for all the groups to meet at a Chinese restaurant in Cambridge on Sunday evenings. Everybody used chopsticks, and the mark of an old pro was to be able to turn your rice bowl upside down after eating and not have left a single grain of rice to fall out. Many years later, when I met my husband, he was prepared to teach me to use chopsticks; he was impressed and, I think, somewhat disappointed that I already possessed this skill.

The president of Wellesley at that time was Mildred MacAfee, who in 1944 was appointed head of the WAVES. This was the female branch of the Navy - a new concept at that time – and she was later able to offer housing to some naval cadets at Wellesley. We doubled up in some of the dorms, and two of the Quad dorms, Casenove and Pomeroy, were set aside for the men. There had been a dearth of men since we started college, due to the war, and it was exciting beyond measure to have them on campus. Of course, intermingling was strongly discouraged, but when has that ever stopped young people from getting together? I remember a step-singing when, to the tune of the then-popular song "Lay That Pistol Down, Babe," the class of '44 sang to us:

> Lay that lipstick down, girls,
> Lay that lipstick down.
> Forty-four will take the floor
> When the Navy comes to town.

They went on, in song, to tell us that we'd have to settle for college boys. We quickly responded:

> Lay that lipstick down, girls,
> Lay that lipstick down.
> You can have the Navy;
> We'll take dates in town.

Going on with:

> Give to us our Harvard,
> Just as you suggest;
> You take over Caz and Pom;
> We'll take all the rest.

After a couple of more verses, we ended with:

> Forty-four is feeble;
> They don't know the score.
> No more competition
> Left in forty-four!

They responded with their class cheer, given in mock-feeble tones as they leaned on imaginary canes.

There were other war-related activities. I particularly recall our sewing room, where some of us would drop in when we had a little free time, working on projects assigned us by the Red Cross. We made baby and children's clothes, as I recall. Many of the girls could use sewing machines, but long seams tended to get erratic, and I soon found that they were often left for me. (I must say that sewing is a skill which has served me well throughout my life. When I was pregnant, I made much of my maternity wardrobe, and when the children were little I made a good number of my girls' dresses and slacks, including huge bells on their bell-bottom pants. Just recently I reduced the size of a quilt from full to single-bed size.)

During my years at college, I often had visitors from home. My sister, then about ten, spent a weekend with me during my freshman year. It was fun seeing her go from Shakespeare to the Bobbsey Twins and back without any apparent awareness of their difference in quality. My friend Edie also came to visit.

I was taking a course in Comparative Psychology at the time, teaching hooded white mice to run a maze. Edie remembers going to the lab with me to feed the rats. It appears that I took the two rats from the cage and put them into her shocked and unwilling hands while I cleaned the cage. I spoke with her last week, and it was an experience she will never forget! As an addendum, it was the female rat who came out ahead in the competition to master the maze. I had named them after characters in Greek myth – Agamemnon and Clytemnestra. Now I inserted a mark of her achievement, renaming the female Clytemnestra Victory Hood. I don't think she cared a bit!

In my pre-Shakespearean Lit course sophomore year, I again met a woman who became a lifelong friend. She was a freshman, and I first noticed her because of her notebook, on which was inscribed her full name – Marguerite Veronica Mary McInerney. It was an enormous name for such a little person, and with her permission I shortened it to Peggy. And Peggy she remains to me, though Phil, her husband, later renamed her Maggie, a nickname which has been adopted by most of her friends. She was a day-student, a resident of the town of Wellesley, and I enjoyed dinner at her home from time to time. Though superficially very different, we share values and principles, and have remained close and mutually supportive friends for over sixty-five years. I was a bridesmaid at her wedding, and we have visited back and forth throughout the years. She had six children, (yes, she is a practicing Catholic) and the first time I invited her family to visit, she said, "You don't understand, Sis. *Nobody* invites a family with six children to visit!"

I was fortunate in having relatives in the Boston area. I occasionally saw the Sharonsons, cousins of my father, who lived and (both) practiced dentistry in Brookline. But it was my mother's aunt, Tante Shiva, to whom I felt closest. Tante Shiva lived in Everett, sharing a house with her three daughters, a son and a grandson, my cousin Alan. When I had the time, I loved going there for dinner and to visit with people whose love for me was so evident. They were my mother's only maternal relations and as such were of special importance to me. My elder daughter, Sherry, is named after Tante Shiva.

Perhaps this is a good time to mention the samovar! This was a gift to my mother's maternal grandfather from a grateful Jewish community, after he had led a contingent of townspeople to an interview with Czar Nicholas II in an effort to negotiate better treatment for the Jews of that area. For some reason – perhaps he had only daughters – it became family tradition that the samovar was to go to the oldest daughter in the family. Mother came here as a little girl, but when she later met her aunt, Tante Shiva presented it to her. Mother's mother, who died at my mother's birth, was the older sister, and Tante felt it was rightfully Mother's. It came next to me, and I have already passed it on to Sherry. Recently I told my grandchildren the story, and the question was asked, who gets it next? Auntie Sherry has no children. So I asked, "Well, who is the oldest daughter in the next generation?" Tessa's eyes got very big, as she pointed to herself and asked in an awed voice, "Me?" Her astonishment and delight were a joy to behold!

My college class included some very interesting people, several of whom had connections to wealth or politics. Just in my freshman dorm I remember one woman whose father was a well-known politician, another whose name was that of a famous candy manufacturer. There were others whose names represented considerable wealth. But I particularly remember Nayantara Pandit, whom we called Tara. She was the daughter of Madame Pandit and a niece of Nehru, both major leaders in an India which was not yet free of British domination. As such, she and her sister, a Wellesley junior, were sometimes invited to British Embassy affairs. I recall her telling us of one such affair at which a young officer complimented her, saying, "Miss Pandit, how lovely you look in your native costume." (She was, of course, wearing a sari.) She responded courteously, "And how handsome you look in yours!"

Dating was not a large part of my life at the time, and I had no 'boyfriend' to ask to my senior prom. But an old friend of my brother's, Herb Rivkin, was home from the Navy; he and I had been good friends, and I was pleased that he accepted my invitation to be my escort. Herb was always a fantastic dancer, and I wasn't bad myself; in my first strapless evening gown, I had a wonderful time.

Graduation day came at last. My parents thought my lack of energy and somewhat downcast manner were due to regret at having to leave my college days behind. But it turned out that I was running a fever of over 102 degrees during the festivities and went to bed as soon as we returned home. That was probably only the second time that Dad had driven up to Wellesley

Mother used to write to me at least once a week, as I did to them. (Long-distance phone calls were much too expensive for anything but an emergency.) But Dad virtually never wrote. Once or twice a year I would get a long 'poem' written by him – he was very good at doggerel – and I used to claim that he didn't really know how to write prose. I was amazed to learn that, when he was in the Army during World War I, he had written to his mother every day. I wish I still had the letters I sent home; they would provide a good record of my college life.

CHAPTER VIII: OFF TO GRAD SCHOOL

In August I was off on a new adventure. I had been accepted into a psychology Ph. D program at the University of Michigan. My parents had given me a check for $2,500, a munificent graduation gift which would see me through my first year there. I was just shy of 21 years old, the age of majority at that time, and my first opportunity to vote would come in September, a month after I left home. But that was no problem – I knew I could get an absentee ballot. I called the Board of Election to find out what I needed to take with me in order to register. My birth certificate and my high school diploma were required. I was able to find my birth certificate, but not my high school diploma, so I telephoned Mother at work; did she know where it might be? There was a brief pause on the phone, and then Mother said gently, "I think they would accept your college degree as proof of literacy." And they did!

As it turned out, I spent only one year at Michigan, but what a year it was! It was immediately post-war, and the campus was crowded with throngs of returning veterans. After a brief stay in a rented room, I was able to obtain space in a Quonset hut dorm in Ypsilanti, just outside of Ann Arbor. There was a group of twenty-four such buildings, originally built for aircraft workers during the war. Now they were used as dorms for graduate students and returning veterans. With 23 men's dorms and one women's dorm, I had an incredibly active social life. It was the only period in my life when I sometimes had an early date and a late date in the same evening. Coming from a small, war-time women's college, it was beyond amazing. Furthermore, my experience of sports events had been limited to watching Harvard lose to Yale.

Sarai G. Zitter

Michigan was a major sports-oriented university, though, and it happened that we won the title in all seven major sports that year. I attended football games, sat in the cheering section, and loved every minute of it. But I've never cared to go to a football game since.

An incident occurred, amusing in retrospect, during that winter. I woke up with a sore throat, feeling feverish, and called the Health Service for advice. It was midday, and "all the doctors are at lunch," I was told. The receptionist suggested that, when I was feeling better, I should come in and let the doctors take a look at me. I asked, "Just out of curiosity, suppose I were to die before I feel better?" Clearly shaken, she asked, "Oh, is it that bad?" Though I didn't think so, she did manage to give me information about a doctor I could call after hours. It turned out that I had Infectious Mononucleosis and was hospitalized at the Health Service building for several days, where I enjoyed surreptitious visits from some of my friends. The only known treatment was rest and nourishing food, but I recall those days as the only time in my life when I literally had no appetite.

I found the educational program to be somewhat disappointing. At that time - I don't know if it is different today – the program was heavy on psychological testing, in which I was not much interested. I was interested in doing therapy. I'm not sure how deep my understanding of therapy really was, but there was something in it which fascinated me. I might add that it does so still. So, by attending classes over the summer, I was able to organize my courses to net me an MA. in psychology. In retrospect, I'm not sure if part of my disenchantment with Michigan was also due to a romance which ended unhappily; perhaps I wanted to be home to lick my emotional wounds.

During the ensuing year I explored Schools of Social Work, and was admitted to my first choice, Simmons. I also obtained a job as a case aide in the social service department at Mt. Sinai Hospital in Manhattan. This gave me an opportunity to see if social work was really what I wanted to do – and oh! it certainly was. I also worked at Mt. Sinai as a summer substitute for social workers on vacation, during the summer between my two years at Simmons.

My time at Simmons was a major high spot in my life. The learning was intense, requiring as it does the use of one's own personality and belief system. The fact that we were involved in internships from the very beginning also increased that intensity many times over. My agency supervisor, Milton, was a terrific teacher, and his faith in me encouraged me to have faith in myself.

It was during that first year at Simmons that I experienced my first loss by death of someone close to me. Bubby, my paternal grandmother, had always lived near us and had been a constant, loving figure in my life. Now, at age seventy-eight and soon after a fall, she died quietly in her sleep. My brother, who was by that time back at Harvard, arranged for us to fly home together. It was my first time in a plane. Dad didn't trust planes, which were not common until after the war, and had never permitted me to fly. But Barry, home from the war, had no such compunctions, and somehow, after that, flying was accepted for us – though never for Dad.

All of her ten grandchildren were close to Bubby, but I think my six year old cousin Myra felt her loss most keenly. Bubby used to baby-sit for her often while Aunt Shully was teaching. I wrote Myra several times in an effort to comfort her, and that was when the nucleus of what later became our informal Cousin's Club was begun. I pointed out that she and I were the only two middle ones in the family, each having both an older and a younger sibling, and we thereby established The Ancient And Honorable Society Of The Middle Ones. Later we encouraged parallel societies of the Big Ones and the Little Ones, determined by family position rather than age or size. To this day, Myra and I will sometimes address one another as "Middle-One".

But back to Simmons: for my second year I felt fortunate to have the Worcester Youth Guidance Clinic as my fieldwork placement. I have always had a particular interest in children – in fact, my Master's thesis was about abused and neglected children, and I later worked for four years in a shelter for just such children – and this placement was a plum. As it was out of town, it included free housing at the Worcester State Hospital for the three days a week that I spent there. We had social work students there from BU and BC, as well as Simmons, and it was a pleasant social group, as well as a wonderful learning experience. Of course, this housing gave rise to many jokes in the family. When patients asked Dad or Mother about their children, Mother would take great delight in saying that I was at the Worcester State Hospital – "that's a mental hospital, you know." When they then asked if I was working there, she would say, "Oh, no; she just lives there!" Dad couldn't stand it – he always had to explain the situation.

During the days when I was not in Worcester, I lived with my brother and sister-in-law. Barry had gotten married immediately after college - we used to say that he was officially a Bachelor for only a week - and was attending Harvard Law School on the G. I. Bill. Bobbie was attending Perry Kindergarten Normal School – yes, they had Normal Schools in those days, considered a teacher's preparatory school – and I, of course, was at Simmons Social Work. Student housing was scarce, and the best I could find was sharing a very large room with three other girls. Bobbie took one look at it and insisted I move into their spare room.

Bobbie and I had become instant friends when she and Barry became serious about one another. She was only nineteen when we met, and I was twenty-one. We started a close friendship which we enjoyed until her untimely death in her sixties. I think that those days of living together cemented our relationship in a way that might not otherwise have occurred.

How can I adequately describe my days at Simmons? Though we were a tiny school – the combined membership of both classes was at that time only seventy students – we were all on similar life trajectories with similar goals and directions. It felt as though someone had selected a group from among whom I could choose friends, and some of those friends remain dear to me unto this day. I think of Irma, whose home was the first private home (as opposed to apartment) in which I had ever spent the night, and with whom I have shared joys and tribulations throughout the years. We have celebrated the achievement of each other's children, and supported each other through difficult times. I think of Ella who recently died in a nursing home, who demonstrated such strength as she uncomplainingly cared for her husband, sick for many years, and made the life adjustments necessary to raise five daughters on her own. (We also visited back and forth, size of family notwithstanding.) I think of Arlene, who moved to New Jersey when she married and has been a loyal and caring friend through the years. And I think of Dorothea, who might have been constrained by race as well as gender, but who enjoyed a fascinating career with the UN, applying her social work skills to international relations.

Though I enjoyed and respected most of my teachers, there

was one with whom I seemed not to get along – truly a rarity for me. I don't recall the exact subject, though I know it dealt with children, but in my youthful hubris I disagreed with several things she was saying, and did not have the good judgment to keep my mouth shut. Think of my dismay, then, when I saw that she had been named as one of the three examiners for my orals, the major exam which determined graduation. But I had not reckoned on my defenders. Maida Solomon, the head of our psychology department, had a great liking and respect for me - and when I came to the exam, she had been substituted (I'm sure had substituted herself) for the unwanted examiner. My confidence immeasurably restored, I sailed through my orals with flying colors. It was only recently, coming across my college records, that I realized that my passing grade was 'superior'.

CHAPTER IX: WORK...AND LOVE

Social work was an up-and-coming profession at that time, and jobs were going begging. Rare was the student who did not have his or her first job secured well before graduation. The best-paying job for beginners at that time was at the Veteran's Administration, which paid an astonishing $4,200 a year. (Social agencies at that time were paying about $3500 annually for beginners – after six years of college!) I was sorely tempted, but decided I did not want a caseload which might consist largely of passive, dependent men. (How wrong I was about that! And how little did I realize that I might instead end up with a caseload largely peopled by demanding, controlling women.) After interviews, I was offered jobs at both the Jewish Board of Guardians and the Jewish Family Service. Though strongly drawn toward the former, I felt I would get a broader foundation in a family agency, which might offer a wider range of issues with which to deal. In retrospect, I believe that I was right.

The Bronx office at which I worked was filled with young, eager workers, both men and women. Their names are popping up in my memory as I write, along with little stories about some of them. There was Ronnie, a handsome young man who described how a client came in with a sore on his nose, and tried to link it to his feeling that for his therapy he was "paying through the nose". Ronnie suggested that there was also a germ theory! We had Mike, Asian-looking (I believe from Hawaii) whom Ronnie pretended to think was a North Korean; this was, of course, during the Korean War. There was Wanda, a soft-spoken, gentle young woman, who was approached when we were holding a lunch-time picketing demonstration in an effort to negotiate better salaries from the Jewish Federation.

Sarai G. Zitter

A passerby said to her, "You shouldn't worry about money. You should be doing this for love!" Wanda's response was a classic! "I do love my work," said Wanda, "but I also love to eat!"

And then, there was Molly. A graduate of the New York School of Social Work, she had come to this job six months ahead of me. The whole group was friendly and social, but Molly and I became friends almost at once. She has been a significant person in my life ever since, and I in hers. We attended one another's weddings, were like aunts to each other's children, and comforted each other in times of sorrow and loss. It was Molly who brought me into Americans for Democratic Action, and it was through ADA that I met my husband – so we always considered her our 'schotkhin', or marriage broker. Molly remains an important person in my life to this day. We have had theatre subscriptions together for countless years, and her home in midtown Manhattan continues to be my pied-a-terre in the city.

I recently wrote an article for my community news magazine entitled, "He Picked Me Up In A Railway Station," subtitled "How I Met My Husband." Here it is – I have no need to reinvent the wheel!

HE PICKED ME UP IN A RAILWAY STATION
or How I Met My Husband

Had you asked my husband how we met, he would have said "I picked her up in a railway station" – technically true, but nonetheless giving an erroneous impression. Here's how it happened.

The year was 1952. Liberals were massing behind Adlai Stevenson, and my friend Molly had introduced me to a wonderful organization, Americans for Democratic Action.

64

Organized in 1947 by people like Eleanor Roosevelt, Hubert Humphrey and Joe Raugh (AKA Mr. Civil Liberties), it was established to continue the policies of President Roosevelt and the New Deal. A week-long summer workshop was planned at Bard College, featuring top-notch speakers and hands-on training sessions. It seemed a perfect venue for my summer vacation.

Arriving by train, we were met by those who had driven up, including Sam. As he went to put my guitar into the trunk, I demurred, preferring to keep it safely between my knees. Sam claims that that is why he sat me in front, next to him. By the time we reached Bard, our enthusiastic discussions had started us on the road to friendship. We spent much of that day and evening together and agreed to meet before breakfast for a pre-breakfast stroll in the rose gardens. An early riser myself, I had no idea what a major decision that was for Sam, who loved to sleep late

We were not the only ones out so early. In the garden we ran into New Jersey Congressman Charlie Howell, our featured speaker for that day. As he and Sam introduced themselves, Mr. Howell said, "And this is Mrs. Zitter?" As we disabused him of that idea, Sam swears he was thinking, "Not yet!"

Valkill Cottage, Mrs. Roosevelt's personal hideaway, was very near Bard College, and she entertained us all at a picnic there. An extraordinarily gracious lady, she made each of us feel like her special guest. It was hard to believe that we were chatting casually with this incredible American icon.

By the end of the week we were most definitely an item. Sam's best friend, George, came up for the concluding weekend, and I later learned that Sam had said to him, "I think that's the girl I'm going to marry!" But Sam had to go back to work, while I had another week of vacation which I had already arranged to spend at a folk dancing camp in Plymouth, MA. No problem: Sam would join me for the following weekend, which fortuitously was also Labor Day, and we would drive home together. I might mention that Sam later told me he had always thought he liked thin lips in a woman, but once he had kissed me, he realized that full lips were more his type!

Sam was chairman of his ADA chapter in Manhattan. With Election Day approaching, we had no time for normal dates. We spent our courtship on a sound truck for Stevenson, Sam giving political speeches and I, with my guitar, singing political songs, many of which we wrote ourselves. Alas, our candidate lost, but we got to know each other in a way that ordinary dating never could have achieved. I knew that Sam would be visiting his parents in Florida in February and was determined somehow to go along. Fortunately, he proposed in January – almost five months after we had met – so the problem was solved.

An interesting addendum – I had been asked, with my guitar, to provide the entertainment at the New Jersey Roosevelt Day Dinner that January. I had gotten permission to bring Sam, and it was the day after we became engaged. The first public announcement of our engagement was made at that dinner, to a crowd of 200 people, by the evening's chairman – Representative Charlie Howell. (We invited the Howells to our wedding – they couldn't attend, but sent us a copy of The Congressional Club Cook Book, the source of my favorite Apple Crisp recipe!)

Sam was a man of great charm, and I was not the only one aware of it. Girls swarmed around him wherever we went, and at the end of meetings I would sit quietly knitting while he answered their questions and sometimes, I suspect, declined their invitations. But he was also well-liked by men, and his thoughtfulness, innate courtesy and genuine interest in people always brought him friends. He also was very bright, kept up with affairs of the day and always had reasoned opinions to share. He filled the bill so perfectly that I used to say there was a Sam-shaped hole in my heart, just waiting for him.

His proposal on January 24th was pure Sam – "Will you help me to enrich both of our lives for the rest of our lives?" But by then we were both so involved with each other that any other outcome would have been unthinkable. When he brought me home that night, as I was hanging up our coats he leaned over and whispered to my mother, "Of course, the only reason I'm marrying her is to get you for a mother-in-law!" And Mother's response was typical of her; she whispered back, "And if I believe that, you have a little bridge in Brooklyn that you'd like to sell me!"

By then, of course, Sam and my family were well acquainted, and there was already the beginning of the mutual affection and esteem which they felt for one another throughout their lives. But Sam's family was becoming concerned regarding this woman whom he kept telling them about, but whom they had yet to meet. Using a catch phrase with which his parents were familiar, he had told them, "The bells rang!" – so they knew it was serious. In December, before we were officially engaged, Sam's oldest brother came to New York for a visit. I have no doubt that the purpose was to look me over and report back to the family. As Sol was crutch- and wheelchair-bound due to polio as a toddler, he was staying at a downtown hotel rather than in Sam's walk-up apartment, and we met him outside on the sidewalk. As we were chatting, waiting for a cousin who was to join us, I saw a high school friend, Sheldon Jacobson, walking down the street towards us. Delighted to see him after almost ten years, I rushed up and flung my arms

Sarai G. Zitter

around his neck. Sam was confused; such a warm greeting, and he hadn't even introduced us yet! It turned out that Sheldon was the cousin for whom we had been waiting.

I joined Sam on his trip to Florida in February. Of course, both of Sam's parents, as well as his cousin Al, came to the airport to meet us. They greeted me with great warmth and insisted on immediately taking me on a tour of Miami Beach, of which they were very proud. It was almost midnight, and I was exhausted, but I could hardly refuse to go – so I got the run-down on all the new hotels, almost falling asleep in the process. But I was up bright and early the next day, as was my future father-in-law, so Pop and I went off for a brisk walk around the neighborhood. When Sam arose, much later, he was amazed; he had just gotten there, and already his father had eloped with his fiancée.

We had thought about a March wedding, but Sam's parents had a gift store in Miami Beach and could not both have left it during the season. So we settled for May and spent the intervening three months working out all the details of our wedding. We had lots of fun planning it. Sam and I dropped by various weddings and Bar Mitzvahs to check out caterers and dance to different bands, and my mother helped us to evaluate possible venues. As it had to be kosher, we ended up at the Hotel Westover, where Barry and Bobbie had gotten married five years earlier. For those who believe in astrology, an interesting fact: the year we married, 1953, saw my brother's fifth anniversary, Sam's brother's tenth, my parents' thirtieth and Sam's parents' fortieth. Seems even the stars were on our side.

CHAPTER X: WEDDING BELLS

We spent a lot of time planning our wedding, looking for an apartment, and visiting at my parents' apartment. As I've mentioned, Sam and Dad grew up in the same area, but life was very different in their differing generations. Dad told us some of his experiences at the turn of the century when he was about five. For instance, if a car went by, the kids would run after it yelling "Get a horse!" If they chased it for a few blocks, it was almost certain to break down.

I recall one night when we were looking at apartment ads in the Times. My Aunt Shully, who had raised three children in a two-bedroom, one-bath apartment, was visiting when we read out an interesting ad – something like nine bedrooms, seven baths and twenty-two closets. She immediately had a proposition for us: we could have the bedrooms, and she would take the closets and bathrooms!

It was somewhere in this period that we had a special dinner out with Bobbie and Barry, celebrating our engagement and their anniversary. We chose a French restaurant Sam had noticed, Le Coq Rouge. The menu in the window seemed reasonable enough – something like $2.95 for lamb chops, if memory serves. And the waiter was most gracious: "What dressing do you want on your salad? How do you wish your potatoes prepared?" etc. We had a lovely evening – but when the bill came, it turned out that nothing was included, and there were separate charges for salad, vegetables, potatoes, etc. Sam and Barry between them did not have the $36 plus which was called for, and this was before the days of credit cards. Joking about washing paper napkins, Bobbie and I emptied our wallets as well, but to our embarrassment the waiter ended up with a paltry tip indeed.

Planning our wedding, we had to decide between a sit-down dinner and a buffet. The former would cost us $15 per person, while the latter would be only $7.50. As the buffet would allow us to invite more people, we opted for that. We both had large families, and being aged 26 and 30 respectively, there had been enough time for us to acquire lots of friends whom we wanted to invite.

Sam had three brothers, but opted for his friend George Spencer as best man. My closest friend, Ellie, was unable to get in from her west coast home, and I chose my sister-in-law, Bobbie, as matron of honor, and my younger sister, Mira, as maid of honor. (She had by then changed her name from Myra to Mira.) With three hundred guests, the festivities began at 1 PM on Sunday, May 3.

I had decided not to use the rabbi from our family synagogue. I knew he would use the opportunity to speak at length about my father and all he did for the synagogue, and I wanted our wedding to be about us. I chose the father of my friend Judy Baily as our rabbi, and he performed a lovely ceremony. I was not fully aware until much later how difficult that must have been for Dad, but to his credit he did not make a fuss about it. I suspect my mother's calming hand had something to do with that.

My family tends to provide its own entertainment, even at affairs such as this. I recall that at my brother's wedding, he harmonized with my father, Uncle Sambo and cousin Myron on the song, "I Ain't Got No Money" – and my new sister-in-law took the mike to say, "Now he tells me!" At our own wedding we brought my guitar and led some of the singing. We also had another of Sam's cousins, Sheldon Finkle, do some square dance calling. People were having so much fun that it was hard to get them to leave. By six o'clock I had to tuck my gown over my arm and go around the room telling people it was time to go home; the facility needed to get the place cleaned up for the next wedding!

I had found to my surprise that Bachrach, the top photographer at that time, was quite competitively priced, and I was more than pleased with the service they provided. In addition to capturing all the people we had identified in advance, they got quite a few pleasantly unexpected shots. I had banned flash bulbs during the ceremony, but was delighted to find that a time exposure had captured the moment beautifully. A final picture showed Sam carrying me up the stairs, in full wedding regalia. Many years later, when our children looked at this album, one of them remarked, "Gee, Dad, I bet you couldn't do that now." And my husband earned his permanent place in heaven with his reply: "Of course not; I'm much older now!" (That kind of answer was typical of Sam; he was always upbeat and encouraging. Throughout the years, when I complained about gaining weight, he would say, "There's more of you to love." What, then, if I should lose weight? "Then it's more concentrated!")

The buffet was great, but every time I headed for the food table, someone caught me and led me back to the dance floor. Sam and I were both enthusiastic dancers and had chosen a really good swing band. But that meant that I ended up the afternoon still hungry – and the same went for Sam. But not to worry – we had reservations for the night at a fancy midtown hotel; we could get room service.

I had not been prepared for the fact that people would be giving us gifts of cash and checks all during the afternoon. When we got to our hotel room, we ordered dinner and then, while waiting, spread out on the bed to count our unexpected hoard. It came to $965 – an absolute fortune. We deposited it in our just-opened joint bank account the following morning before leaving on our honeymoon.

When dinner arrived, it was more than we could finish. So, thrifty wife that I was, I tucked the remaining steak into a couple of rolls, wrapped them in napkins and put them out on the windowsill to keep cool. Next morning we were awake long before they were ready to start room service. But we had our steak sandwiches, giving rise to what became a watchword between us. In a heavy Spanish accent, Sam said, "Steeck with me, keed – I geeve you steak for breakfast!"

Sam would have liked to go to Mexico for our honeymoon – he spoke good Spanish – but I was not able to get away for more than a week. We decided instead to drive down the beautiful Blue Ridge Highway, but as it was raining all the way to Washington, we opted to stop there and do some sightseeing. Sam had never been to Washington, and we both found it exciting. I had visited before, though not done any real sightseeing. It had been during the war, and a cousin of mine, Isabelle Sharonson, was getting married. Barry was overseas and my parents couldn't get away, so I was designated to represent the family. What I most remember of that trip was starting to get on the bus when I saw the sign, "Colored seat from the rear". Stunned, I backed down from the bus. I certainly had read about segregation, but had never run into it personally….and in our nation's capital, no less. I simply could not bring myself to get on that bus. I stood on the sidewalk, debating what to do. I did not feel I could afford a cab, and it was much too far to walk. Reluctantly, I waited for and took the next bus on which, unwilling to sit in the designated area, I stood all the way.

Sam and I stayed at a newfangled kind of place called a motel, on the outskirts of town. Our room was really a suite, boasting both a kitchen and a dining area. I promptly bought a coffee pot and some breakfast staples, which saw us through the week. I had a college friend living in Washington and a connection of my family worked in some government office. The latter, Asher Ende, took us to lunch in the Senate dining room, and we got to sample the famous black bean soup which, by an act of Congress, is always to be found on the menu.

We were back in Washington in June, as we were to be every year, for the ADA annual Roosevelt Day dinner. As a chapter chairman, Sam was well-known, and introduced me to many people active in liberal politics. But, newly-married, he had a momentary lapse of memory, once introducing me with, "And this is my wife, Sarai Golomb." (In those days, women seldom kept their maiden names.) On our trip home that time, we offered a lift to three young women whom Sam knew from the Chelsea Chapter. We had forgotten that we had never removed the lip-sticked "Just Married" inscription with which my sister had marked our car. Sam began to wish he were wearing a turban, as heads swiveled in surprise at this just-married car filled with one man and four women.

We had found an apartment just a few days before our wedding. It was in a rent-controlled building in the Chelsea area of Manhattan, convenient both for my subway to the Bronx and for Sam's drive to Jersey City. For a good-sized three room apartment, we paid the munificent sum of $85.00 per month, rent controlled. But we felt it needed painting, and that would be our responsibility. One day while still in Washington, we passed a store which had Martin Seymour paints, a very good quality, on sale. In the flush of our enthusiasm, we selected two colors and filled the trunk of the car with our purchase. The colors were chartreuse and what we called bordello red, and what a dramatic contrast they made. Our long entry hall practically glowed, and people were known to wear sunglasses long after entering our home. But we loved it!

We arrived home to find that Sam's parents, who had stayed in our apartment while we were gone, had not tactfully removed themselves before our return as we had anticipated. They decided to stay to greet us – so when Sam carried me across the threshold, it was into the waiting arms of my new mother-in-law! But they had already made arrangements for accommodations elsewhere, and left soon after we arrived.

A cousin of my father's, Aaron Gross, had given us six sets of the sterling flatware pattern we had chosen – but our china had not yet arrived, so I used the silver with paper plates when I served dinner that night. Actually, for many years that silverware, its numbers augmented by other wedding gifts, was the only flatware we owned. (I have always been a believer in using, rather than saving, my good things – after all, who is more important to me than my family? – and silver doesn't break.) After dinner that first night, we sat on the couch for some serious smooching – until I jumped up, saying – bridelike? - "Excuse me, dear; I have to throw away the dishes!"

When we were shopping for a silver pattern, Sam was stunned by the prices, which averaged about $21 for a five piece sterling place setting. He told me that in China he could have gotten a set of three-piece silver place settings, service for twelve and with his initials worked into the handles, for about twenty-one dollars….but he thought it was too expensive!

Sam had been pleased with the painter who had done his previous apartment, so we called him for an estimate on ours. Pedro and Sam greeted one another effusively, speaking in a cross between Spanish and English which I could only partly follow. Apparently Pedro wanted $100, and Sam kept pointing out the things he would *not* need to do, such as ceilings and closets, and negotiated him down to $70.

The apartment was duly painted and was truly dramatic in the vibrant colors we had selected. When Pedro came to be paid, Sam – delighted with the job he had done – gave him a $30 bonus, bringing the total back to $100. But the story has another chapter. While we were eating dinner that night, there came a knock at the door. There was Pedro, holding out $30 and saying, "Your husband made a mistake; he gave me too much money." I assured him that my husband had given him exactly what he intended and that we were delighted with the job he had done. That was the first of many times when I realized that Sam had negotiated down a price just for the sheer delight of being able to do it.

CHAPTER XI: MARRIED LIFE

Sam worked in Jersey City and I in the Bronx, so I almost always got home earlier. That was fortunate, as I was the one who loved to cook. Sam had had his own apartment for six years before we married, so he knew better than most young men how much needed doing in a household. We were both good at compromise and cooperation, and an easy routine was established.

Unlike most young couples in those days, we were not pressed for money. When we announced our engagement, Sam's annual income had been moved up from $5,500 to $6,000, while I was earning a great big professional salary of $3,900. Sam commented that when he was a boy, he had thought that if he ever earned $10,000 in a year he would be a rich man – and now, with the help of his wife, he was almost doing it.

We took up a suggestion my mother had made regarding finances. Both of us were frugal by nature, and we were saving for a house. Mother suggested that we keep track of every penny we spent for the first year or so, in order to know exactly where our money was going. We had categories set up in a little notebook, and it was actually fun noting absurd little details like carfare or a magazine. But it was useful; we discovered that we were spending an inordinate amount on entertainment. As we analyzed it, we realized that we were going out much as we had done while single. We began inviting friends for dinner instead of meeting them at a restaurant, and they would naturally then invite us back. Our entertainment budget dropped sharply.

We did eat out occasionally. Sam's favorite neighborhood restaurant was the Boulevard de Paris, and I still recall his favorite dinner there – the London Broil Special which, including salad and dessert, came to $1.87. I might mistrust my memory, but it is recorded in that early ledger.

There were adventures, or at least amusing incidents, as we set up housekeeping. I passed a grocery store on my way home from the subway and found that I was introducing Sam to vegetables which were, to him, previously unknown. One such was Brussels sprouts. In my family we always had referred to them as fairy cabbages – I had a very creative mother – and when I saw them in the market, I suddenly couldn't remember their real name. I could hardly ask for fairy cabbages – so I pointed and said, "I'll have a pound of those!"

Sam and I each had a very different sense of time. I was quite precise about time; if I had expected him to pick me up at seven-thirty, I would have been ready at seven twenty-eight and tapping my foot by seven thirty-one. But Sam's attitude toward time was much more casual. He didn't allow for the extra moments of getting ready or getting someplace. He might tell me he was going to be out for an hour, because he expected to spend an hour with the person he was seeing. He forgot about going downstairs, walking to his car, driving ten minutes cross-town to reach his destination, and going up in the other apartment building – and then the same when returning home. Thus an hour could often be an hour and forty-five minutes, a problem if we had other plans.

As I've mentioned, Sam had a car. I had a driver's license but hadn't driven in so long that he gave me a refresher course. My original driving instructor, however, had been my brother. Dad really didn't think women needed to drive and never considered letting me use his car for practice. But when

Barry came home from the service, he bought an old Chevy and did so much work on it that we considered it to be an original Golomb. When he drove it between Cambridge and New York, he carried a five gallon container of water with which to replenish the radiator a couple of times en route. Barry was a very good, very patient teacher, and I believe I was an apt student. We never got into a hassle over it, and I was soon ready for my driver's license exam. I couldn't take it in Barry's car – it never would have passed inspection. Dad refused to let me use his, the explanation (excuse?) being that it needed always to be available for emergencies. I'm sure my mother had a little talk with Uncle Sambo, for he offered me the use of his car for my test. To practice, I drove his car when the family went out to visit the cemetery in Long Island. I couldn't believe how easily it responded. I had assumed that Barry's car bucked when I started it because I was such an inexperienced driver; I didn't realize that it behaved itself only for Barry. Uncle Sambo's car started right up smoothly, and I passed my license exam without incident. Sam was an equally patient teacher, and my children will attest that I was the same many years later when they were learning to drive.

In many ways, Sam and I had rather an easy time adjusting to married life. We had spent so much time working together, politically and otherwise, that we found fewer surprises than is often the case. Also, we shared so many values and interests, and were each so ready to compromise, that the bumps smoothed out with surprising ease. We shared our attitudes toward family involvement, toward saving and spending, and toward what was important in a home and in life. Sam was almost too obliging; he had learned while young that it only created hurt feelings when he disagreed with his mother, and when we disagreed he was quick to say, "You're right." But I didn't want to be 'right'; I wanted us discuss our differences until we arrived at a mutually satisfactory solution. I think that the effort he put into learning to express those differences of opinion was helpful to him at work throughout the years.

We had a lot of fun shopping for furniture, even though our apartment couldn't hold much of what we would eventually need. Sam's work with Lightolier involved a lot of decorating and style awareness, and he had entrée into many of the better furniture houses in the city. I knew little about style but loved the modern furniture which reflected his taste. When I was little, I hated dusting the openings and curlicues in my parents' traditional furniture and vowed that when I had a home of my own I would buy only smooth, easy-to-dust surfaces.

Our dining alcove was just five feet square, and we bought a table to fit. It was 22 by 42 inches when closed but opened to 72 inches to seat eight. That table went through several incarnations during the years, including as the children's play table, eventually winding up as the surface on which to keep the cat's food out of reach of the dog. Sam and I both loved company, so of course our living room couch was a sleeper. Our kitchen was so tiny that we could not pass in it without rubbing up against one another – but that was just fine with us!

After a couple of years in which we remained active in ADA, we decided the time was right for starting a family. I had become unintentionally pregnant soon after we were married, but had an early miscarriage. As I was not yet ready for children, I was not as troubled by that as I might have been – but when I again miscarried two years later, I was devastated. Would I ever be able to have a healthy baby? My wonderful obstetrician, Dr. Luschinsky, assured me that there was nothing wrong with me and suggested we try again right away.

During the previous year I had visited two of my friends

in the hospital right after they had given birth. Irene had her child at Doctor's Hospital and described the experience as wonderful! She had been anesthetized as soon as she arrived and didn't know another thing until she woke up in her room. They had promised to bring her the baby later that day. Flip also had a wonderful experience. She was at French Hospital, in the rooming-in section. She had natural childbirth, no anesthetic, and was able to watch the procedure in a ceiling mirror. She had the baby with her at all times and nursed on her and the baby's own schedule. Each of my friends thought her experience the best possible one, and I reflected on our good fortune in having so many options available to us. Of course, Flip's experience was the one I wanted to emulate, and my first two children were also born at nearby French Hospital, attended by the same doctor as was she.

Because of my two earlier miscarriages, I was ordered to bed for my entire third month of pregnancy. Though I had intended to work until late in my pregnancy, I now arranged to work part-time for a couple of weeks, closing out my case-load, and then obediently went to bed. Sam took the opportunity to buy a television set, which I had always vigorously opposed; he insisted that I would need it for entertainment during those long weeks in bed. It was installed in the bedroom, but I don't believe I ever turned it on when I was alone. Sam always brought me coffee in bed before he left, and I was permitted to get up for lunch and to use the bathroom. You can imagine how relieved I was when I entered my fourth month, past the danger point, and was again permitted to resume my active life. But with no job, my do-it-yourself tendencies came to the fore, and with my trusty sewing machine – Sam's first Valentine's Day gift to me after we were married – I went to work. I made receiving blankets, hemmed heavy diaper cloth as a cheaper alternative to buying diapers, and knitted like mad. I made a lovely little white and mint green sweater and hat set for bringing the baby home from the hospital; it looked as though it would barely fit a large doll. But it brought all three of my babies home and eventually wound up being used, indeed, for a doll by my children. I knitted a carriage cover too, and I don't remember what else. When I was allowed to go shopping, I delighted in putting together a wardrobe for a new infant. Sam, who had always been a much more enthusiastic shopper than I, went with me for the minimal furniture we were buying, such as a carriage and a changing table. We never did buy a crib; Aunt Shully gave us the apartment-sized crib which she had used for her three children, and when we later moved to a house in New Jersey, one of Sam's Remson buddies from City College passed on a full-sized one. I have always loved painting, and both of those cribs went through a variety of decors before they were eventually retired from service.

I had read Dr. Grantly Dick Reed's book, "Childbirth Without Fear," and was determined to be awake and aware during what I knew would be among the most exciting, rewarding experiences of my life – no anesthetic for me! I attended classes and exercise groups at Maternity Center and could hardly wait for my due date of November 10th.

My monthly checkups went well, and my weight gain was within normal limits. French Hospital was only ten blocks from my home, so when the question came up of how I would get to the hospital if Sam were at work, I cheerfully declared that I would walk. My doctor said, "Fine- but be sure to take along a policeman or a New York cabbie, just in case the baby doesn't wait!" I got the message and promised to call a cab!

As it happened, I went into labor during the night of November 10th and woke Sam by three A.M. to help time the contractions. We waited till six to call the doctor, who promised to meet us at the hospital. First babies typically take a while to come, and it was well after noon before Sherry arrived. We had remained for some time in the labor room, as Dr. Luschinsky was waiting for the delivery room with the best ceiling mirror. The nurse was getting upset: "Doctor, the baby will come right here in the labor room." Dr. Luschinsky was unfazed. He said, "Well, nurse, you're here, I'm here, and Mrs. Zitter is here; if the baby comes to join us, that will be just fine." I had a bad moment when the nurse insisted on taking my eyeglasses; how would I watch the birth? Again, Dr. Luschinsky came to my rescue. He said, "I'll take care of them, nurse," and pocketed my glasses, only to return them as soon as we got to the delivery room. In those days, fathers were not allowed at the delivery, and Sam was very sad at being excluded.

I cannot describe the thrill of seeing that little dark-headed creature pop out, red and squalling. That her lungs were healthy was obvious. They wrapped her in a blanket, put her on her stomach in a rolling bassinet, and an hour later were wheeling her down the hall alongside my gurney as we headed for my room. This just-born child gave a preview of her personality: her head was up, and she was looking with interest at the world around her – at one hour old.

The rooming-in unit supported breast-feeding, which fit into my plans. The baby was taken to a nursery at night so that I could sleep without interruption, but was with me at all other times. When my pediatrician-father came to see me for the first time, he naturally gave her a thorough going-over. When he came back to my room and I said, "Isn't she beautiful?" he looked startled. "I don't know; I'll go look," he said, proceeding to do just that. He came back and agreed with me, of course. His first concern had been to check for anomalies of health or development; looks had not even occurred to him.

People used to ask if I had a preference for a boy or a girl. I didn't, really. However, everyone so assumed that I would want a boy first that it gave my stubborn nature a slight preference for a girl. I wanted four children; Sam wanted two. We eventually compromised on three. I was afraid that if my second were a boy, having one of each, Sam would want to stop there – so I had a slight preference for another girl – and, of course, got Mark. Then, when it turned out that my third would be so close in age to Mark – only seventeen months apart – I thought it would be easier caring for them if they were of the same gender…and I got Robin. Fortunately none of those preferences was more than a passing thought, and I always felt like a friend of ours who had adopted her children. "I thought I wanted a boy," she told me, "but if they had put a little girl into my arms, I would have wanted a girl!" Somehow, babies tend to bring their own welcome.

I think I had an easier time dealing with infants than do most new mothers. First of all, I was not a kid – twenty-nine when Sherry was born. But more importantly, I had helped in Dad's office, holding babies and doing various small tasks with them from adolescence on, so I was very familiar with their care. Sam's and my differing sleep schedules came in very handy; an early riser, especially after having the baby, I tired early and would often be in bed by eight-thirty or nine. Sam usually was at his desk till close to midnight, so he would change the baby's diaper and bring her to me in bed for the night feeding. It was so cozy snuggling with that warm little bundle, and so gratifying to be able to satisfy her needs.

I remember one funny situation. I had a bad cold, and when Friday night came, Sam insisted that I must sleep late the next morning. He was hard to wake up, but made me promise that I would roust him out notwithstanding, and he would care for the baby. Gratefully, I promised. Next morning, Sherry 'went off" like clockwork at the usual 6:30 A.M. I pushed Sam; I prodded him; I reminded him that he planned to get up with Sherry. "I'm getting right up," he assured me, dozing off again. After several tries, each time with his insistence that I stay put and he would take care of things - followed by a snore - I put on my robe, changed Sherry's diaper, fed her, entertained her for a while, and at nine o'clock put her down for a morning nap. As I slid back into bed beside Sam, he turned, threw an arm over me and declared, "Don't move a muscle; I'm getting right up!"

When Sam and I first were married, some people predicted that our differing sleep patterns would prove a problem for us. As a matter of fact, it often was an advantage. In earlier days, Sam would take the night shift driving home, while I would sleep in the car. I handled morning chores – dragging him out of bed for work, as well as taking care of coffee, breakfast, bed-making, etc. He would take care of any evening tasks, though he used to work at the desk, both for Lightolier and for ADA and the Democratic Club, until very late. Now that we had a baby, his late nights and my early mornings meant that someone was awake and available for her most of the time.

Memoirs of a Fortunate Life

CHAPTER XII: A HOME OF OUR OWN

When Sam first mentioned looking for a house in the suburbs, I was surprised. It had never occurred to me to live anywhere except in layers between other families, as one did in city apartments. But I began to see the advantages of such a move as I realized that I would have to have my eye on Sherry every minute if we stayed where we were. Also, we were clearly outgrowing our apartment. Our friends were thinking in the same direction. Sam, who always figured the angles, thought that if we went to a builder and offered to buy several similar houses at the same time, we would get a discount. We were a group of four couples – my brother and sister in-law, Barry and Bobbie; our best man and his wife, George and Muriel Spencer; Bosh and Irene Stack (Bosh and Sam had been on their college newspaper together), and Sam and me. We spent many Sundays looking at houses and plans, and realized that builders were already putting up whole subdivisions and would not be at all impressed by our pitiful little group. We found a house in Metuchen which we all liked, but as we tried to pin down our plans, it became apparent that we all required different locations. Within a couple of years we all had bought houses – but George and Muriel ended up on Long Island, Barry and Bobby in Ardsley, NY, Bosh and Irene in Nanuet, NJ, and we in Cedar Grove.

I had told Sam that if I were going to give up the advantages of the city, then I wanted the advantages of the country. We found a wonderful, expandable split level, with a back-yard overlooking reservoir property. Because of this, we knew that our view would be preserved; no one could build behind us. It was adjacent to a bird and small game sanctuary, and our children used to feel they had a six hundred fifty acre back yard. Actually, our own property was a level three eighths of an acre, and I became an avid gardener. We were, like everyone else in those days, pinching pennies, so I learned to root cuttings; I bought tiny baby shrubs, sometimes for as little as twenty-five cents apiece, and planted them far enough apart for eventual growth, meanwhile filling in the spaces with bulbs and flowers. How did I learn all this? I talked to experts, I asked lots of questions, and most of all, using my typical means of getting information, I 'looked in a book'. Several books, in fact. Additionally, our neighbors across the street had a resident grandfather, an old Italian farmer. I picked his brains a bit, too. (But it was in snow shoveling that I learned the most, just from watching him. No matter how heavy the snow, he carefully marked out a small section, just big enough for his shovel to get under, before lifting it and tossing it aside. If the snow was deep, he took only the upper part of his section, returning for the rest. In this way he never overtaxed his back or his heart.)

We moved to Cedar Grove on November 9, 1956, just two days before Sherry's first birthday. We threw her a birthday party, inviting our friends and relatives who sat on cartons of books and rolled-up carpets. That was the only time I ever didn't bake one of my children's birthday cakes – that task was undertaken by my mother. We luxuriated in the spaciousness of our six rooms. You can imagine how crowded we had been when I tell you that the furniture from our apartment was almost sufficient to fill our new home. The upstairs had our bedroom, with a full bath, no less! – plus two other bedrooms, one for Sherry and the other to serve as guest room until we had another child. There was no den – the big two-sided desk which we had designed was in the living room. There was also an unfinished playroom and basement, as well as a two-level attic, with the lower portion ready for finishing. Sam said this was our first five-year home. We moved out thirty-nine years later!

The movers, in addition to taking the furniture from our apartment, had made two other stops. They got my harp from my parent's apartment, and from storage they picked up an upright piano which we had 'inherited' from a friend of my grandmother. During the ensuing years we inherited lots more furniture – including a chest of drawers from Uncle Sambo and Aunt Faye, a storage chest (from whence I don't recall), and the cribs I've already mentioned. I also received a walnut cedar chest on legs, circa 1915, which had been an engagement gift from my mother to her older foster-sister, Aunt Sarah. Minus the legs, it still stands at the foot of my bed, as beautiful as ever.

My parents-in-law had made a pact with one another when I was pregnant with Sherry; if I had a boy, Pop would come up for the Bris. If it turned out to be a girl, Mom would come up. (They couldn't both leave the store during the season.) So Mom had been there the previous year, and now Pop came up to visit and, he thought, help us to move. He had seen the baby, of course, as we had trekked down to Florida the previous Passover – baby, car-bed, disposable diapers and all. They had arranged diaper service for the week of our stay – the only time when I did not wash diapers myself. In the new house, there were the usual unexpecteds, the most difficult being that the heat had not been turned on as promised. With an elderly man from Florida, as well as an infant, this presented a problem in November, but fortunately we were able to get it solved before anyone froze. But setting up housekeeping while wearing gloves does present a challenge.

The first snowfall came a few weeks after we moved in. At three that afternoon, I received a call from my mother. "Sis," she said, "Be sure to get out there and shovel. Don't leave it till Sam gets home. Men are much more prone than women to get heart attacks!" I laughed as I told her that I had already shoveled – but then asked, "By the way, just who's mother-in-law are you, anyway?"

We were still part of the great post-war emigration from city to suburb. Moving as we did into a new development, we found many young couples, all – like us – looking for friends for themselves and playmates for their children. The Goepels on one side had three boys – eventually, five children – and the Tanises on the other side had one girl, just Sherry's age. Eventually they also ended up with five, including two boys Mark's age and a girl in Robin's class, so just our three houses provided membership for a football team. There were children all up and down the block and throughout the development. As time went by, we could open the door, and our children had friends and schoolmates in every direction. It was also a highly ecumenical group. We quickly met and became friendly with neighbors of all persuasions. There were Catholics on one side of us, Dutch Reform on the other, and an assortment of Jewish and Protestant representatives scattered beyond. Our block was fairly inter-ethnic, with people of Italian, German, Dutch and English backgrounds mingling comfortably. Only one color, though – a fact of which we became increasingly aware as Civil Rights activities heated up during the following years.

As I mentioned, we were the proud possessors of three eighths of an acre, lightly seeded with grass but having no shrubs other than a few miniscule foundation plants. We knew it would take time to get it into shape, but were eager to get started. That first spring we invited our relatives to, not a garden party, but a gardening party. Aunts, uncles and cousins arrived with trowels, bulbs, seeds, and various other bits of gardening equipment. Blue-jean clad, they set us up for a colorful spring to tide us over until we could develop a proper planting plan. I learned later from an across-the-street neighbor, Betty, that she had watched the arrival of all the cars, with people tumbling out and hugging one another, with a wistful nostalgia. She wanted to run over and get in on the hugging herself. Her family was Italian, and this was just the way they used to get together. "But," she explained, "we live near Bill's family now. They're English – we shake hands!"

At a garden center that first spring, I decided to splurge with a bunch of pussy willows. The American kind, with small gray catkins, ran to thirty-five cents a bunch, while the French pussy-willows, with large pinkish catkins, cost seventy-five cents. Feeling reckless, I sprang for the French variety. To my astonishment, they rooted in the vase, and I planted them in the back yard. They eventually became a shrub ten or more feet high, and cuttings from that bush provided French pussy-willows all throughout the neighborhood. A well-spent seventy-five cents indeed.

Although the property on which our house stood had once been farmland, the builders had followed the common practice of selling off the topsoil, leaving us with very poor planting soil. That first summer, Sam toiled every weekend and many weekday evenings, digging out the earth around the house to a width and depth of almost three feet and replacing it with topsoil. As I was the family gardener, this was a real labor of love on his part, with me as the beneficiary. Sam took care of the grass and occasionally the trees, and of course was always there to help if a task was too heavy for me alone, but I was the one who fell in love with gardening and pursued it as a major hobby for most of my life. Quite a change from watering a few plants in my fourth-floor apartment!

Although he entered our lives somewhat later, I must here mention Mr. Wissing. Living in Montclair, he had a very large back yard which he turned into an evergreen farm. He rooted and grew a large variety of evergreen shrubs, and I was able to stock up on tiny seedlings literally for pennies. Twenty-five cents was a typical price for a baby shrub, and I remember splurging – only once – for a somewhat larger one, which set me back a whole two dollars. We planted them far enough apart to allow for eventual growth and filled the in-between spaces with flowers and bulbs. Later, to celebrate Robin's birth, he gave us a yellow firethorn in her honor.

Of course, we also invested in deciduous flowering shrubs. There was a lilac bush at a front corner. Sam was disappointed that it didn't bloom right away. But one day he returned from work to find it ablaze with fully-grown lilacs. Though thrilled, he also was a bit suspicious; how could this have happened so suddenly? Well, my mother had come to visit and brought a bunch of lilacs. I scotch-taped them to the branches of the little lilac bush, which was barely strong enough to bear the weight and Presto – instant bloom!

The idea was not original. Some years earlier, when my mother had expressed regret that it was taking their apple tree so long to bear apples (my parents had by this time a country house in Lake Peekskill) my brother and sister-in-law had taped apples to the tree, and then continued to tape apples to the grape arbor and the rose bushes as well. Continuing the tradition, when Mark's birthday turned out to be in the summer, a lollipop tree grew each year just in time for his party. Starting as a bare twig, for a week it got bigger and more multi-branched each day, until on the morning of his birthday party it was ablaze with varicolored lollipops. The guests, of course, picked the sweet fruit on their way home.

Within a year or so of moving to Cedar Grove, I became pregnant again. Always robust, I gave little thought to my miscarriage history and continued with my active schedule. One morning, after having helped Sam move soil in our front garden the previous day, I once again lost the pregnancy.

Though of course disappointed, I was not nearly as distressed as I had been the previous times; I was pretty confident that I would be able to have other children, and this time, of course, I already had Sherry. In retrospect, all those miscarriages were a blessing! If I had not had the first two, I would have had somebody else – but not Sherry. And had I not had the third one, I would have had somebody else – but not Mark. It is unimaginable to me that I could have missed out on having just exactly the children that I did have.

I soon became pregnant again. Having had such a satisfying experience with Sherry's birth, I decided to use the same doctor and hospital for this second time around. I left Sherry with various neighbors while I traveled to New York for my monthly doctor's appointments. And when I went into labor with Mark, my friend Helen came to stay with her until my mother could come out by bus and bring her back to the Bronx for the week. Once again I had just the kind of delivery and hospital experience that I wanted. Mark looked entirely different from Sherry as he emerged from the birth canal. He was blond to her darkness, skinny to her roundness. He also quickly subsided into sleep; the world didn't bother him a bit. I had rooming-in, and by the time we went home from the hospital, I knew he was of a different temperament.

Sherry and my mother came with Sam to the hospital to pick me up. We had earlier prepared a bassinet for the baby, and a smaller one for Sherry's doll. We also had planned that Mother would carry and tend the baby, so I could be fully available for Sherry, who had not seen me for five days. But when we came downstairs, Mother sat alone in the waiting room, while Sherry was so involved in figuring out how the hospital switchboard worked that she hardly gave me – or Mark – a passing glance.

When Mother learned that I had a boy, she had immediately

purchased a boy doll for Sherry and spent the ensuing several days knitting and sewing a wardrobe for it. To decide on a name, Mother went down the alphabet with boy's names – Alan, Bernard, Charley, David – until she reached Ricky, and Sherry said firmly, "That's it!" So Ricky he became, and he accompanied her to the hospital. When we arrived home, I set the baby down in his bassinet – and Sherry put Ricky into the little bassinet nearby. I asked, "What makes you think that's for Ricky?" Sherry smiled wisely. "I know!" she assured me. "I know."

Sherry embarked with great gusto upon the task of being a big sister. Mark was an easy-going infant – quite different from Sherry, who had been colicky, keeping us walking the floor at night for hours. He was one of those children of whom one says, "You wouldn't know there was a baby in the house!" But on those occasions when he did fuss, Sherry was there instantly with a pat, a toy, or – imitating her mother – a song. She also decided that she was now too big for diapers – at 2 years and 8 months old. She was already dry by day, and I promised her that when she had three dry nights in a row, she could stop using diapers altogether. Bright and early three days later, I saw her carrying a stack of diapers from her room into Mark's. "These are for the baby," she said – and was dry thereafter.

Another 'toilet-training' incident came some two or more years later. Sherry needed the toilet urgently; she ran upstairs to her usual bathroom, but her father was using it. On she rushed to my nearby bathroom, only to find me occupying it. So down she sped to the playroom bathroom, two floors below. Describing this hectic dash, she said, "When Mark gets too big for the potty, we'll have to build another bathroom!" Thinking back to the single bathroom in my family of five, not to mention Sam's experience with a hall bathroom shared with other families, I assured her that we could struggle along with three!

Sherry had been an unusually early talker. If I did not have it written down, I would doubt my recollection – but she was speaking in grammatical paragraphs soon after she was two. I recall going under a bridge which spanned the highway, when she was just past two; she asked what it was, and I said, "An overpass." As we approached the next bridge, she said, "Look, Mommy, there's a –" then corrected herself to "There's *an* overpass." Sam, with no special experience of young children, did not realize how unusual was Sherry's early and correct language. When Mark was almost two and had barely begun sentences, let alone paragraphs, I found Sam one day regarding his son with great sadness. "He's such a sweet little boy," he said. "What a shame he's never going to be smart like Sherry." I was outraged. "When he graduates from college, I'm going to tell him you said that," I declared. And when Mark was graduated Magna Cum Laude from Wesleyan, I did just that!

When we originally discussed our plans for a family, I wanted four children and Sam wanted two. (After some of the colicky nights with Sherry, he wondered if one might not suffice!) Good compromisers that we always were, we settled on three. At one point I considered pushing for seven, so that we would compromise on four – but I knew I'd never get away with it. Sooner than we had planned I was again pregnant, and Robin's arrival followed Mark's by a mere seventeen months. I thought it would be easier to handle two babies in the same room, so with much fanfare Sherry and Mark changed rooms, he now getting the larger one to share with the new infant. We made a big deal about Sherry's new 'big girl' room, as well as the grown-up bed which replaced her youth bed. Mark was too little to move out of a crib, but we inherited a full-sized crib, which I repainted for him, so that he also had a new,

' big-boy' crib, leaving the smaller one (also repainted) for Robin. Actually, we put it up in the attic for the last couple of weeks of my pregnancy, so that when it came down again it was his "old, baby crib."

I remember my brother-in-law Itch stopping by while I was crib-painting. Without removing his shirt and tie, he picked up a paintbrush and worked along with me, never getting a spot on himself. As I was rashly painting the uprights a different color from the horizontal bars, it was rather a delicate undertaking.

Robin entered the world three weeks later than expected. I had decided that returning to New York was too much of a hassle, with two young children already at home, so I found a doctor in Montclair who was ready to help me with natural childbirth. One of the hospitals at which he practiced was planning to start a rooming-in unit in the near future; as I had already had this experience twice before, they agreed to let me have the baby with me, so I was able to enjoy her full-time presence, just as I had with the others. With Mark so young, I cut my hospital time to the minimum allowed, and was home four days after giving birth. I was sure Robin was a girl before they even told me – from the top, she looked exactly like Sherry.

I had gone into labor at 6 A.M. This time we had Sam's Aunt Mollie and Uncle Sam coming out to stay. Childless themselves, they were warm and loving people, and they adored our children; we anticipated no problem. Once again, my friend Helen came to stay until the family arrived, and Sam rushed me to the hospital. After delaying until three weeks past her due date, she was in a tremendous hurry to be born. The doctor examined me and said it would be a little while yet – and I suddenly felt the baby beginning to emerge. I cried out, "I think it's coming." The doctor told Sam to grab the other end of the gurney, and they rolled me down the hall to the delivery room. Sam asked, "May I stay?" and the doctor asked, "Will you faint?" When Sam assured him that was not a risk, he said, "Sure!" – and Sam had the privilege of seeing his daughter enter the world! At that moment, I think he was even more thrilled than I.

In those days, children were not allowed in the hospital, and seventeen-month-old Mark in particular missed me dreadfully. When I came home, he followed me around for days, never letting me out of his sight. And poor Aunt Mollie: when she came to visit, he broke her heart by wanting nothing to do with her as he clung to me even more tightly.

Sherry's big sister role expanded, and she took it seriously. I made a point of proving that I could fit all three of them onto my lap at one time, but she found it more comfortable to sit next to me on the sofa, holding Mark in her lap; she called herself the "little Mommy," and obliging little Mark seemed satisfied with the arrangement. I always felt fortunate that she was my first; she set such a wonderful pattern of kindness and helpfulness for the others to follow. Of course, it was not always followed; Mark tended to poke at the girls when seated next to them at the table or in the car. In fact, our places at table were set by that; Sam was at the head, I next to him on the side nearest the kitchen, and Mark next to me. The girls were across from me, with Robin next to Sam for occasional assistance and Sherry next to her in the lefthander's position. In later years I was amused to see them always take those same positions, even though Mark no longer poked his sisters and Robin no longer needed help in cutting her food.

While not as assiduous at it as Sherry, Mark did take his older sibling role seriously. He was concerned at what he perceived to be Robin's slow development – after all, she could neither walk nor talk! – and was quite dissatisfied with my apparently laissaiz-faire attitude toward the matter. When she was about a year old he, 17 months her senior, decided to remedy the situation. I came down to breakfast one morning to find that Mark had helped Robin into her feeding table, gotten out the mug covered with animal pictures, and was trying to teach her to talk. I arrived in time to hear him say, pointing, "Now, Wobin, say 'jawaffe'." My only thought was, "If he's the one to teach her to talk, she's in for a bad time."

Mark's speech continued to need improvement, and when he was in school he received help for his first couple of years from the speech teacher, Miss Bates. He would be assigned homework that involved cutting out pictures that started with a specific letter, or grouping words in some fashion. The whole family sat around the table working on these projects with him. When Robin got to kindergarten, however, she felt deprived; nobody was giving *her* any special projects to do. I had a word with Miss Bates, who promised to take care of it. She called Robin into her office, had her repeat words and phrases, and then said, "Oh, Robin, what beautiful speech you have. You don't need my help at all." And Robin was satisfied.

I wonder if my children remember Mrs. Fay. I needed additional help after Robin was born and hired a middle-aged Irish woman who, having raised her own seven children, had flexible time available. Her father, who lived in Ireland, was clearly in decline, and she wanted to earn enough money to go back and see him. The house really sparkled under her care – I've never been much of a housekeeper myself – and it was amusing to come home from shopping and see Sherry and Mark lined up next to her, washing walls or wiping counters. She was enormously impressed by my education and profession, and I later learned that she prefaced much of what she said to her adolescent children with "Mrs. Zitter says…." Three days a week gradually lessened to three half-days, and ultimately to one day a week, but Mrs. Fay was with us for four years. When she left, she went to work for the city of Newark, and it was there that she learned the value of my having insisted on paying her Social Security. She had not wanted that, as it meant that her income was reported, and hence taxable. But in Newark, working with other clerks, she understood that ten years in the system would reward her with a small income in old age – and her four years with me put her almost halfway to that goal. To her credit, she made a point of calling to thank me.

CHAPTER XIII: FAMILY AND FRIENDS

During all this time, we were of course seeing a lot of our families. We spent most of the Jewish holidays with my folks in the Bronx, though when Pesach fell during the children's vacation, we would trek to Florida to share the Sedurim with Mom, Al and Sol. Pop had died during my pregnancy with Mark – Mark is named after him – but we saw a lot of his brothers and sisters in New York. Although some of them were a bit odd, they were a loving, caring family, and along with the aunts, uncles and cousins on the Golomb side, they enriched the lives of all of us. My parents were only an hour away, so visits with them were more frequent, but we made it to Florida for a week each year, Pesach or not, and Mom usually spent at least a week with us during the summer, with Sol and Al coming from time to time as well. I had been raised in a home with elastic walls, and Sam and I continued in that tradition. Family and friends knew they were welcome, and when we exceeded the bed capacity, our children gave up theirs and slept on the always-available floor.

When visiting my parents for a holiday dinner, I would usually drive in with the children, while Sam would take public transportation from work to meet me there.

Traffic was sometimes horrendous, and on one such night, when Sherry was about four and a half, Mark two and Robin an infant, only very quick reflexes avoided an accident when a car in the left lane darted across in front of me to reach an exit on the right. Those were pre-seat belt days, and my arm shot out to keep Sherry from flying against the windshield. I didn't realize until later how shaken she must have been.

I arrived in New York to find no available parking space

near my parents' home. Spotting my Aunt Mollie walking over to join us for dinner, I sent Sherry and Mark up with her, needing to cope only with Robin's carriage when parking several blocks away. When I reached my parents apartment, I heard this story: when the children arrived with Aunt Mollie, my mother asked Sherry, "Is Mommy parking the car?" to which Sherry responded, "Yes," then added gratuitously, "My Mommy is not a very good driver!"

We were sorry that, living over an hour from Barry and Bobbie, our children did not get together as often as they and we would have liked. But Bobbie and I worked out a system to somewhat minimize that problem; periodically we would meet at a highway rest stop about half way between our homes, bringing Sherry and Ruth with us. We would have coffee and visit for half an hour, and then one of us would take both girls home, only to swap again after the weekend visit was over. The girls were good friends and continue so to this day. One Chanukah, they even arrived at the family party wearing identical dresses, purely by happenstance.

Ruthie, who has a lovely singing voice, has also continued in her mother's footsteps as a talented seamstress, later adding quilting to the mix. Bobbie used to make most of her own clothes, as well as those of her children, and Ruthie has quilted some remarkable pieces. I have an elegant wall hanging which she made, and each day I enjoy putting across the foot of my bed the beautiful quilt which she gave me on my 70th birthday.

Our friends were, of course, raising families and settling into new homes, just as were we. Although we continued much visiting back and forth with them, as well as with Barry and Bobbie, we made some good friends near our new home as well. Closest of all was Helen, my neighbor two doors down the street. Older than I by seventeen years, I was as near the age of her daughter Lexie as I was to her, but we became the dearest of friends. Helen had a car, but because of a painful shoulder, she hated to drive. I, carless, loved driving, and we explored the neighborhood together.

I'll never forget our first meeting. I had accepted the job of collecting for the local United Way, thinking it would give me a chance to meet all of my neighbors. Fifteen-year-old Lexie came down as I was talking with Helen, inquired if I had children, and told me that she baby-sat, and that she loved children. Helen said, "It's true, Lexie loves children. She also loves money." I knew right away that this was a woman I would enjoy getting to know. As it turned out, Lexie was our favorite baby-sitter for several years to come. In fact, when Sherry was a toddler, she called every teenage girl with long hair a Lexie.

Helen was an Early Childhood Development specialist. She directed a nursery school, and when I later started a co-op nursery school, she was our unpaid professional advisor. We shared values and philosophy, and had great respect for one another, as well as a deep affection. Although she later moved to Massachusetts, where she directed the state's Head Start program, we remained very close until her death at age eighty-four. When she developed cancer and needed a mastectomy, I drove up after the surgery and brought her home to care for her and supervise her recovery. Some years later I helped her plan her move to a nursing home, and hers was the first of three funerals which I have been privileged to conduct. Sherry reminds me that, just after college and while looking for a place to live in the Boston area, she lived with Helen for a while.

Another good friend was Rita. She had a daughter in Sherry's class and a son in Robin's, so we were able to do a lot together. It was a loss for me when her family moved to Connecticut, but unlike most of my friendships, this one did not survive the separation, and to my regret we have essentially lost touch.

I have a tendency to throw myself wholeheartedly into whatever activity I undertake. It was thus with civil rights; it was thus with feminist issues; and it was thus with the co-op nursery school. Sherry had attended nursery school at the Community Church. Outgoing, self-confident and gregarious, the class of twenty-four children proved no problem for her. But when it was Mark's turn I knew that, despite the three teachers, the sheer size of the class would overwhelm him. In those days, it was the rare middle-class woman who worked when she had small children, and with encouragement from Helen, I put together a group of young mothers who formed the board of what would become the Cedar Grove Co-op Nursery School. It was an all-consuming activity, as we wrote articles for the local newspaper, collected toys and blocks, books and puzzles, meanwhile painting melon boxes and shelves to hold them. I was board president, and we hired a professional teacher-director and wrote a constitution and by-laws. A co-op nursery school uses the parents as assistant teachers, not only saving money but also exposing the parents, instructively, to a group of other children of similar ages. Parent education is a part of the plan, and this was my responsibility. I am proud to say that not only did this school serve Mark's and Robin's needs, but more than twenty-five years later was still in operation.

Sam and I were do-it-yourselfers, and quite creative both at saving money and at adapting things to our use. I had made most of my maternity wardrobe, and now in our new home I made drapes and curtains for most of the rooms, using the living-room floor as my worktable. I've already described some of our major gardening activities, and they continued throughout our lives. I was always the gardener for shrubs, flowers, bulbs and vegetables, while Sam cared for the lawn and the trees. But our boundaries were always fluid; Sam helped with heavy yard work, and – to the dismay of some of my female neighbors – I often pitched in on the mowing. (Mark was a summer baby, and in my maternity tops and shorts, I was quite a vision behind the lawn mower. I believe I looked rather like a kewpie doll.) Later on, on weekend days in the spring when I was laboring in the garden, I would hear that welcome call, "Come on in; lunch is on the table." and find that my darling husband (sometimes with the help of one or more children) had indeed taken care of that chore.

With three children in four years, I could be pretty exhausted by the end of the day and often was in bed by 8:30 or 9:00. Sam, working at the desk, would try to deal with infant needs without disturbing me. Always creative, he tied a string to the bassinet and replaced the wheels with rockers. Thus, without looking up, he would pull the string, rocking the contented baby while he accomplished his paper work.

A word about that desk. We had seen one which we loved at Herman Miller's showroom, but knew we would not have room for two of them. So we found a fine furniture maker and designed our own, based on the one we had seen. But this one was two-sided; we sat opposite one another, each with a bank of drawers on the right, and with a middle drawer which went right through. Many times, as Sam did work he had brought home from the office and I dealt with bill-paying, we would send each other love-notes via that center drawer!

I loved being home with my children during their pre-school years. Although it was the norm, many women found it tedious and stifling. For me, able as I was to keep myself stimulated by engaging in a variety of political and social-service activities, it was a joy to be there for first words, first steps, and to see all the exciting little changes that take place in a child's early life. In fact, I often felt sorry for Sam, not being home to participate in all of this. But despite being an active participant in their lives – he was a loving, devoted father – he was glad to be off to the greater stimulation of his work. A science fiction fan, he once suggested that there should be a device whereby children could be put into cold storage until they were six or seven, and you could hold real conversations with them. I was outraged; think of all the fun we'd be missing!

It has always intrigued me to realize how old we must seem to our children. I recall Sherry once asking, "In the olden days (sic) when you were young, did they have spinning wheels?" "Yes, dear," I assured her; "in all the museums they had spinning wheels." Many years later, when the children were in high school and studying about the second world war, they were impressed but somewhat shocked when I added information which had been current events for me. I suddenly realized that I must have seemed as old to them, speaking of my war, as my father had seemed to me when he spoke of his.

CHAPTER XIV: BACK TO WORK – AND AGNES!

Much though I enjoyed those days at home, I was eager to get back to work, and as soon as Robin entered first grade, I was ready. It felt important to be with them while they were home, but I had no devotion to housekeeping as such. Somebody had to wash and, in those days, iron their clothes – but it didn't have to be me. However, we had no school lunch program, so I needed someone to be home for them on a daily basis. And that led to one of the most luxurious periods of my life.

Full-time help seemed the best answer, and I found an employment agency with the unlikely name of "Fit For A Queen" which brought girls from other countries to do domestic work. Many of them came from South America, but I – who have always been bad at foreign languages – wanted someone who could speak English. It would cost us $150 a month, plus room and board – pretty much all that I would be earning. We settled on a young woman from Scotland, Agnes Hysop, and after several exchanges of letters, we were off to the airport to meet and bring her home.

As usual, Sam and I had done the work of building a room for her – a ten foot square at one end of the playroom – putting up a wall, installing the door and closing off an alcove to make a closet. It took us a long weekend, during which the children were at my mother's.

We had gotten a picture of Agnes, and when she appeared at the airport gate, eight-year-old Mark broke away from us to run up and kiss her. "There," he said. "That was your first kiss in America!"

Agnes was a wonderful addition to our family. We had trouble understanding her accent at first – I began to wonder if we spoke the same language after all – but that soon cleared up, though there were a few amusing incidents. I remember a supper dish she made for the children when we were going out – I thought she called it "toys and men", but eventually we discovered it was "toties and mince", meaning potatoes and ground beef. Although I did most of the cooking, Agnes helped with the preparation, and of course took care of the dishes. I had explained to the children that she was there to help me, as I was spending so much time now at work, but they still were responsible for their regular chores.

Speaking of chores, we had an interesting interchange with Mark in that area, leading to one of what I call my "Mean Mommy" stories He was around eight when he came to me one day to tell me that he didn't think he should have to do things like washing dishes; that was girl stuff. I was in a bit of a quandary: On the one hand, that kind of thinking didn't go in our family, and my feminist hackles began to rise. On the other hand, here was a rather quiet, shy little boy between two much more articulate, assertive sisters and I didn't want to squash his growing sense of masculinity. So I said, "Well, in our family we don't make those distinctions. You know that I do yard work and mow the lawn and help in the workshop, and that Dad helps with dishes and sometimes fixes meals and tidies up the house – but you would prefer some more boy-type jobs, is that it?" He agreed, I'm sure thinking that, as the outdoor season was over, there wouldn't be any for quite some time.

Well, what's the first job we tend to think of for a boy? Taking out the garbage, of course. So, each night, when we were finished with the kitchen clean-up, he was to take the garbage from under the sink and deposit it in the big can in the garage – and twice weekly he wrestled it down to the curb before school and brought the empty can back on his way home.

The can was about as big as he was, and he confided to me that he didn't mind taking out the garbage, but "I really don't like the smell." I had news for him: nobody likes the smell.

The novelty soon wore off and I found myself reminding him night after night. "In a minute," or "as soon as this program is over," or "when I finish this chapter," etc. One night, after Mark had gone to bed, I found the garbage still under the kitchen sink. A few days later the same thing happened.

I've never believed in nagging. I also think that we learn better by action than by words. So the next time I found garbage under the sink at 10:30 at night, I went up the two flights of stairs and awakened Mark. Handing him his bathrobe, I directed him to go down and empty the garbage pail. Mark, always a heavy sleeper, was bleary-eyed – "Hunh? Hunh?" – but staggered after me and did as he was told. When he turned to go upstairs again, I stopped him, reminding him that a clean bag needed to go in the pail. Somehow, the garbage problem was solved!

There is a post-script to this story. Many years later, when I was leading a parenting group in my professional capacity, I told this tale as an example of actions working better than words – demonstrating both natural consequences rather than punishment and a way to avoid falling into a pattern of nagging. One young mother asked, "Did he ever forgive you?" The thought had never occurred to me, but I promised to ask him. He had no recollection of the incident – but he certainly turned into a responsible young man!

We all grew to love Agnes. Our original contract had been for one year, but she stayed with us for four, until she got married. As her own father couldn't come to the States for the wedding, Sam gave her away – though at the last minute he said he'd rather keep her! When she came to us, and we were discussing what she might want to do in her time off, I mentioned reading – and she indicated that she never read for pleasure. Yet a few days later I came home to find her curled up on the couch reading Jane Eyre, which had just been released as a movie. When I said, "I thought you said you never read," she said, "Oh, but this is good!" I soon realized what a very intelligent young woman we had here. Had she grown up in my home, she probably would have been in college at this stage of her life. To the children, Agnes was much like an older sister, and we all enjoyed having her with us. But to me, having her there was sheer luxury!

Agnes had a cousin who was working in Teaneck, and often they would each take the bus into New York to spend their time off together. Much, much later Agnes told me of their first such meeting. It was in the Port Authority bus station, and they stopped at a café there to talk. Her cousin ordered tea, but Agnes asked for a cup of black coffee. "Here just a week and already you're ordering black coffee?" asked her cousin. "Oh," said Agnes, "you wouldn't believe how bad Mrs. Zitter's tea is!"

This seems like a good time to introduce Frisky. We were always an animal-loving family, especially with dogs. When Sherry was about eight, we decided that the children collectively were old enough to take most of the care of a pet, and all five of us visited the local animal shelter with adoption in mind. Among the many barking and yapping dogs we saw a year-old pup gazing at us with soulful eyes. He appeared to be a cross between a German shepherd and a collie – probably a sheltie, considering his small size. Somehow, we all felt drawn to him, and when we returned home we had a pet.

Now we needed a name. We decided to give the children a little political experience, and explained how proportional representation would work. We made a list of names, any suggested name being included unless someone hated it, in which case it was discarded. Then we each voted for our first, second and third choices, giving each number a point value. The lowest number won, and Frisky had a name. Actually, Buster came in a close second, so that was given as well, and he officially became Frisky Buster Zitter.

We have had several dogs, but Frisky was surely the most remarkable. He had a strong herding instinct – no doubt inherited from his collie forebears – and so was a great help to me. When I called the children, he would round them up and bring them home. But he clearly saw himself as one of the children. I had a bell which I rang to call the children in for lunch. When he heard that bell, he was the first one at the door.

He was very easy to train and would walk at heel without benefit of leash, even across the forty mile an hour road nearby. In fact, the only time I used a leash was for his annual visit to the vet. Seeing the vet's building was his signal to take off at high speed. But normally, he was extraordinarily well-behaved. He would sit quietly while I spoke with someone, then follow at heel when I started walking again.

One day Sherry came in, much excited; I had to come quickly; Frisky was going down the slide! I laughed; dogs don't use slides. But I came out as requested, and lo! – there was Frisky standing in line with the 'other' children. When his turn came, he climbed the steps, ran down the slide and then ran to the end of the line once more to await his turn. It turned out that my children had decided to train Frisky as a circus dog. They had first gotten him to jump through the swing (the "flaming hoop") on demand. Then came the slide: they put a dog biscuit on a step just out of his reach; to get it, he had to put his hind legs on the bottom step. Then the treat went one step higher, and so forth. Before long, he was a regular part of the slide play-group.

There is an addendum to this story. A couple of years later, we were visiting my cousins Judi and Lee, whose children were a few years younger than ours. As we sat chatting, suddenly we heard a terrified scream. Two- year- old Michael had gone down their small slide, and then looked up to see what must have seemed a huge monster running down the slide after him. Of course, it was just Frisky, joining in the game as usual.

There was another incident in which Frisky played a major part. To understand it requires a bit of background. Our next door neighbor, a boy Sherry's age, was raising white rabbits. His rabbit had a litter of ten, and he labeled them with a magic marker, putting a number in each right ear. He was selling them for a dollar and a half apiece. Our children were desperate to buy one; they wanted to pool their allowance money for that purpose. We already had a dog and a cat; Sam feared they would not look after a rabbit and its care would fall on me. How, they asked, could they convince him? If they only had the rabbit here, they would show him how well they cared for it. Sam asked if they could rent it for a week, just to see. They asked Walter, and for the princely sum of fifty cents we had a week's worth of rabbit. We put it in a shallow box filled with shredded newspaper, and of course it was a foregone conclusion by week's end that Marshmallow was a member of the family.

There was only one problem. The rabbit appeared to have

some kind of mange – at least, its fur was always wet and sticky. I put her box up on the table to remind me to phone the vet…..and the problem cleared up by itself. It seems that Frisky had adopted the bunny; he thought he was her mother, and was constantly licking her. When she was up out of his reach, her fur dried white and fluffy.

Now came the question of purchase. Sam asked if they had rented with option to buy. What was that? Sam explained, and they agreed to find out. So they asked Walter: did they rent with option to buy? What was that, he asked, and they explained. He agreed that they had! So the transaction was completed, and Sam and the children built a hutch where the rabbit could live out of doors. In addition to feeding her, they felt she needed exercise and would often take her out of the hutch to run around on the grass, nibble at weeds, and generally enjoy a little freedom. But when they were ready to put her back, she would hide under the bushes. That's where Frisky came in. He would nose her out of the bushes and herd her back to the hutch.

One morning, very early, we heard a great barking and scratching at the back door. I ran down in my night clothes to find Frisky jumping against the back door and barking furiously. Following his gaze, I saw a big white rabbit in the middle of the lawn; Marshmallow must somehow have gotten out of her hutch. I opened the door, and Frisky was off like a shot – and then a strange thing happened. Just like a cartoon dog in the movies, Frisky braked to a halt a few feet from the rabbit, turned and wandered off. We went to look and found Marshmallow still in her hutch; this was a visiting rabbit, obviously escaped from next door. And Frisky had given us all a lesson in minding our own business. He had said, clear as day, "It's not my rabbit! Let 'em catch their own rabbits!" "Not my rabbit" became something of a watchword in our family. I have told that story to clients who felt responsible for controlling their immediate world, and more than once have had a client later say something like, "I was going to get involved, but I realized it wasn't my rabbit." And my daughter Sherry, also a therapist, has experienced the same reaction.

Another Frisky story involves Agnes. Our affectionate little dog would lunge at anyone coming to the door, eager to greet them with passionate licks. One day Agnes answered the door, holding tightly to Frisky's restraining collar, to find a disreputable-looking man standing on the mat. "Does that dog bite?" he asked fearfully – to which our quick-thinking Agnes responded, "Only when I tell him to!"

Frisky loved playing with the children, ours and others. When Robin started school, he was suddenly bereft of playmates. Somehow, he managed to slip out of the house, and we had a call from our neighbor, Betty, who had two younger children. She had opened her front door to find Frisky sitting there, a paw outstretched in greeting; he was saying as plainly as possible, "Can Billy and Betty come out to play?"

Naturally, Frisky joined us on our many camping trips. We had a station wagon, and the children and dog were all tumbled together in back. As we shut the car doors, we used to recite the mantra, "Mind the fingers, mind the toes, mind the tail and mind the nose." On one trip, after having stopped for gas, someone suddenly asked, "Where's Frisky?" and to our shock, he was not in the car. Somehow, he had been left at the gas station. Sam turned at the next light and headed back, while I walked back on the side of the road we had been traveling, fearing that Frisky would run into the road when he saw the car returning. When we got back to the gas station, there sat Frisky, calmly waiting for us. We used it as an instructive lesson for the children in case they ever got separated from the family. Frisky knew just what to do, we told them - he waited right where we had last seen him, knowing we would eventually return for him.

There were other occasions when I used our pets as mentors or examples. Mark hated to wash up before meals – why couldn't he just wash the palms and fingers, instead of the whole hand, and certainly the face needn't be clean. I pointed to the cat, noting that even the cat knew enough to wash its face frequently. Mark felt betrayed; "Stop that," he told the cat; "stop that!" And Robin, who felt deprived because everyone in the family wore glasses but she, was comforted when I pointed out that neither the dog nor the cat wore them.

There was another instance when I used the dog – or, at least, our treatment of him – as an example for Mark. I tell it with some trepidation, for today it surely would cause me to be charged with child abuse. Our children were allowed to roam the woods, but there were two rules: I had to know that they were going there and they had to have a companion. There was a family with three little boys who lived nearby. They were rather undisciplined and would take off into the woods on impulse – and six year old Mark would get caught up in the excitement and run off with them. I spoke with him once, twice, three times – I absolutely had to know when he was going into the woods – and then it happened again. I sat him down and reminded him why we kept Frisky on a line - it was so that we could know where he was and keep him safe. Mark was so much more valuable to us than Frisky; it was so much more important that we know where *he* was and that we keep *him* safe. So I tied a long rope around his waist, with the knot at the back, and tied the other end to a tree. Then I went inside and watched through the window. His friends were intrigued; they hung around for a while, but then went off to do other things. (I later learned that the Tanis boys, awed by the situation, had said to their mother, "We're *never* going in the woods without telling you first.") Mark wound the rope around the tree a few times, and eventually sat down, bored, After a few minutes I came out, asked him if he thought he could remember to tell me before going into the woods, and removed the rope. That is another of my Mean Mommy stories – but the problem was solved, and we never got involved in the endless nagging which I feel is so destructive to a relationship. I trust the statute of limitations for child abuse has run out.

CHAPTER XV: OUTDOOR LIFE – AND BEARS!

As Frisky was about a year old when we got him, we have no idea of his life prior to that time. But from the first, he was always terrified of sudden loud noises, and would run to hide under the ping-pong table during thunderstorms. It was this fear which ultimately led to our loss of this beloved pet. He was about five when he went camping with us in western New Jersey at the beginning of Fourth of July weekend. Always well-behaved and responsive to being called, he usually slept under the camper at night, protecting our territory from encroaching squirrels and birds. On July 3rd, someone nearby set off some premature fire-crackers. Though I was out of the camper like a shot, it was too late – Frisky had taken off at high speed, and we never saw him again. We changed our vacation plans and stayed on for several days; we advertised in the local papers, called all the local police stations and animal shelters, but never heard of him again. We tried to take comfort in the thought that, as he would sit and offer his paw to strangers, he must have made friends and found a new family, but we nonetheless mourned his loss most bitterly. For the next couple of years, whenever we heard a sound at night, Sam or I would go downstairs to make sure it wasn't Frisky finally coming home. It was only several years later, when we could feel sure he must already have died, that we stopped worrying about his being in an unhappy or abusive situation.

I mentioned camping; this was our family's preferred style of vacation during the children's early years. When I first suggested camping, Sam was not at all interested. My recollections were of hikes and sleep-outs with my mother and brother in the Palisades. Sam's were of sleeping in the mud of China, sans tent, during the war – an entirely different sort of nostalgia. But, always a good sport, he was willing to try it and soon became an enthusiast.

Many of our family stories date to those days on the road. We camped our way down to Florida one year to visit my mother-in-law, taking along our teen-aged nephew, Wes. On that trip, we covered the whole of aviation in just a couple of weeks; on the way down we visited South Carolina's Outer Banks, where the Wright brothers experimented with their first airplane. And on the way back we stopped at Cape Canaveral – now Cape Kennedy – to watch one of the first moon shots. One night during that trip, we were unable to find the camp ground which we were seeking. It was late at night when a police officer led us to what he assured us would be a good overnight spot. We awakened to the sound of chattering and discovered that we were smack in the middle of a college campus, with students passing our camper in all directions. Sam and I were debating where to go and how to wash, when campus-savvy Wes said, "Follow me!" and led us to a public building where we could use the rest-rooms.

Another side benefit of that pre-seat-belt trip was that all the kids – our three plus Wes – were piled in the rear of the station wagon, where Wes taught the others to play bridge. He and Sherry also wrote a song which they called "The Toll House Blues." When we complimented them on how good it was, Wes replied, "It ought to be; it took us more than twenty minutes writing it!"

A favorite camping trip, one which we took several times, was down the Blue Ridge Highway to the Great Smokies. We have several bear stories which date from those trips. One time, when the children were asleep in the camper, and Sam and I were sitting by the fire, a bear entered the circle of light. For the first and only time in my life, I stepped behind the protective bulk of my husband as I murmured, "Honey, there's a bear." At that point Shadow, our new collie pup, woke up and began to bark. The six hundred pound bear took off at a run, while we laughed to think how embarrassed he would have been to know he had been routed by a five-month-old puppy.

That was also the trip during which we all went swimming in a seemingly bottomless swimming hole. Shadow did fine as long as he felt solid ground under his feet, but when the bottom fell away he panicked and did what any baby would do; he climbed on top of his mommy – me! Sam was not a good swimmer, and I had several anxious moments before I managed to push Shadow off me and struggle us both to shore.

Another time, again in the Great Smokies, we learned that bears were entering camp grounds and stealing food. The rangers recommended making as much noise as possible, banging on pots and pans, to scare them away. It happened that Robin had been studying the cornet that summer. As an incoming high school freshman, she wanted to play in the marching band and knew that the harp just wouldn't cut it. So she had checked with the band director, found that they needed a cornet, and – typical of Robin – set to work learning to play it. When we saw a great crowd at one of the camp sites, we hurried over and were astonished to see a bear sitting on the bench at the picnic table, calmly eating the meal which the family had laid out for itself. The banging of pots and pans had no discernable effect on him. Robin raced back to our nearby campsite, grabbed her cornet and quickly rejoined us. As she emitted a loud blast on the cornet, the bear jumped from the bench and hurried off, to the great applause of the assembled campers. From then on, we referred to the cornet as "Robin's bear-scare!"

My interests have always been many and varied. Girl Scouting, a major interest during my youth, resurfaced as I became a scout leader in the troop that Sherry joined. I had trained and worked as an assistant leader in my pre-marriage days and my love of the outdoors and experience at camping stood me in good stead. I passed my interests along to the girls, and we had many hikes and overnight camping trips together. One hallmark of these outings was our optional sunrise hike. Those girls who wanted to join me would put a white sock conspicuously at the foot of their sleeping bags, so that I would know whom to awaken. Then we would dress quietly and tiptoe out to enjoy the dew on the grass and the sun just peeking over the hilltops nearby. We would take a short pre-breakfast hike, sometimes spotting an early rabbit or bird, and return starry-eyed from the quiet, the peace, the sheer delight of these fresh-scented mornings. These became very special moments for us all.

Another specialty of my troop was our "silence hikes." The girls were used to having transistor radios constantly on the go – but I banned these from our trips. Instead, we would take paper and pencil, walk quietly into the woods, and write down whatever we heard in the silence. The girls developed a good ear for bird calls and what we thought were small animal rustlings, and discovered – to their amazement, I suspect – that they could find interesting new experiences even in the non-electronic woods.

I became something of a community outdoor expert, teaching fire-building to my scouts and map and compass reading to other scout leaders. Our troop met at the elementary school, and I used my guitar to get the girls to arrive promptly. After all, we had pre-meeting singing until everyone arrived, so the earlier one arrived, the more singing time one had. We also developed into a singing troop, and I was delighted to resurrect many of the songs from my own scouting days. Sherry was as enthusiastic a scout as I had been, and Girl Scout Camp was also a part of her summer experiences. I was sorry that Robin never cared much for scouting, though she always did enjoy hiking and camping.

I might mention that Mark was a cub scout for a year; the Boy Scout troop which he then wanted to join met on Friday nights, and as his pre-Bar Mitzvah years were coming, and he would need to attend services at least a good deal of the time, I could not allow that. He was not interested in any other troop, so his scouting career never got off the ground.

CHAPTER XVI: SOCIAL ACTIVISM AND SOCIAL WORK

Throughout the years there have been two major causes into which I have thrown myself unreservedly. Civil Rights was the first of these issues, and both Sam and I were active marchers, speakers and contributors in this area. I started our Fair Housing Committee in my living room, and we integrated the all-white town of Cedar Grove, starting with the house my friend Helen was selling. I had met an interracial couple at a meeting of CORE, the Congress On Racial Equality, and learned that they were house-hunting in our area. It should have been easy to work out the deal. I was surprised at how resistant some of my neighbors were to the idea of a racially mixed couple on our block. Fortunately, Helen stood firm, and the purchase went through. The Stanleys, our new neighbors, had children much younger than ours and Sherry was often their baby-sitter.

Our involvement was international as well. In the fight against apartheid in South Africa, many of the major liberal organizations took turns in picketing that embassy. Representing ADA, Sam and I took our turn the weekend of the ADA national convention. As expected, we were arrested and handcuffed, along with a couple of dozen others. The 'paddy-wagon' was too small to hold us all, so while we waited our turn we were singing protest songs. I kept throwing out new verses to We Shall Overcome, until we finally stopped for breath. The police officer guarding us said, "Keep going! You're the best group yet!" Again as anticipated, the judge let us go on our own recognizance, and we returned to the convention amidst much enthusiasm and cheers.

Those were the days of many major marches in Washington, and Sam and I were frequently in attendance. We had the privilege of hearing Martin Luther King's famous "I Have A Dream" speech from bleachers not more than a block away. I had been hesitant about whether we should both attend that march; we had three young children, and nobody knew whether or not there might be violence. But in the end we couldn't stay away. Was I fearful? Not really; when I was with Sam, I was always ten feet tall.

My other major area of involvement was that of women's rights, most particularly reproductive rights. It is hard to realize today that even contraception was still illegal in Connecticut until 1966. The 1973 Roe v. Wade decision should have marked the end of the battle for choice, but it turned out to be only the opening salvo. I became involved with a group called New Jersey Right To Choose, and before long was visiting schools on its behalf, talking to high school classes about reproductive choice. Of course, the so-called pro-lifers – I prefer to call them anti-choice – were also invited to speak, and I loved to have them go before me. They were so rigid and judgmental that the kids, who of course hated to be lectured at, were all primed and ready for what I had to say. It was always interesting to me that the boys tended to be more anti-choice than the girls. I tried to help them see how this affected them as well; paternity is a lifelong responsibility, both emotional and financial.

I became president of NJ Right To Choose, a position I retained for about twenty years. It involved a lot of public speaking, to adult groups as well as in the schools, and in many ways I feel it helped define who I was. I also represented New Jersey ADA in Choice, NJ, the pro-choice umbrella group consisting of such organizations as ACLU, League of Women Voters, several Jewish women's groups such as

NCJW – any group which included a pro-choice plank in its mission. Together we set the agenda for pro-choice activities in the state. I had many occasions to testify in front of the state legislature, as we took on issues such as parental notification prior to abortion, a conscience clause to exempt pharmacists from filling contraceptive prescriptions, and sex education in the schools. Those were heady times, and despite the enormous amount of time and effort we put in, we thought we could see enough progress to make it all worthwhile. I must admit that, in retrospect, I'm somewhat less sure!

I haven't spoken much of my professional activity, yet that was a major factor in my life. As I said, when Robin was ready for first grade, I was ready to go back to work. I was wondering about school social work, as it would give me the same holidays and vacations that my children enjoyed. I wrote to the County Superintendent of Schools to ask about qualifications, and before I had even received a reply from him, I received two offers of jobs; trained social workers were that scarce at the time. Also, New Jersey had a law, since used as a model for the national law, mandating that each public school have access to a social worker as well as to a psychologist. But while I did obtain my School Social Worker license, I decided instead to work at Essex County Overbrook Hospital, a county mental hospital in Cedar Grove, about six minutes from my home. I was able to work three days a week and spread it over four, from 9 to 3 three days and from 9 to 1 on the fourth, so that I got home almost as soon as did the children. I had not worked for the previous eleven years, of course, since my pregnancy with Sherry. But I found that in the six minute drive each day I made the shift from Mommy to professional, and on the way home did the reverse. And of course, having Agnes there meant that I didn't have the worries of most working mothers of young children; I was covered for illness, snow days and emergencies. I might mention that working part-time and paying Agnes full-time, I didn't come out ahead financially – but oh! how I loved my work. And it did pay off later, putting me several years further along on the pay scale when I finally did work for a school system.

As the hospital offered a county position, I had to take an exam. I sent in my application, but while I was waiting to be notified of the exam date I received notice that I had passed it with flying colors – my score was "Superior". It turned out that my "E and E" – education and experience – qualified me to be hired as Senior Social Worker. That was the easiest exam I ever didn't take!

I learned a lot at the hospital, and as I had a Masters in psychology as well as my MSW, I was invited to join the psychology department in many of their extra trainings. I got my start in Group Therapy at that time, though I later studied it in a more extensive course. But mental hospital work wasn't really what I wanted, and after four years, when Robin was in fifth grade, I got a job at the West Essex Family Service. Doing that kind of therapy – with couples, with individuals, with parent-child situations – has always been my métier, and I have been happiest when that was the center of my professional life. I worked less than a mile from home, so if Sherry – who by now was driving – needed the car on an evening when I was at work, she could walk over and pick it up, and I could easily walk home.

A word about Sherry's driving: as her birthday is in November, she started driving classes at school in September, and I took her out for practice several times a week. It happened to be a rainy fall, and Sherry was involved in many after-school activities, so our practice was often in the rain and as darkness was approaching. One of the first times we went out, Mark asked to come along. I said that was up to Sherry, and she agreed – on the condition that he promise not to say a single word. He promised – and he kept his promise! However, he lay down in the back seat with all three seat belts fastened around him, shivering and moaning in apparent abject terror. He was not invited along again!

The day of Sherry's driving test dawned bright and clear. Sherry was uneasy. She told me that, with all her rain-and-darkness experience, she was not sure she knew how to drive on a bright, sunny afternoon. Needless to say, she did fine, and my only regret was that she had just a year of helping me with the family driving before she was off to college. I might add that, unlike many parents, I was always happiest when it was my own child who was doing the driving, rather than another youngster. I had explained to each of them that the driver's license meant that the State of New Jersey considered them safe enough drivers to drive on its roads. But before they went out alone, I had to consider them safe enough to drive *my child.* I trusted their judgment, and they all turned out to be excellent drivers.

Sherry had once asked, when she was about ten, when she could get a car of her own. I said, "When you have enough money to buy one, and enough income to support it." "What if I have enough money to buy one and enough income to support it, before I have a license?" she asked. When I questioned why she would want a car she couldn't yet drive, she thought a moment and said, "Well, I could lend it to people." So I added a third requirement: money to buy it, income to support it, and a valid New Jersey license. But with access to my car, at age seventeen she no longer felt the need for one of her own.

That car was something special. For many years we had managed well enough with just one car, which Sam usually drove to work. Once a week, he took three busses so that I could have the car, and I did my best to schedule all shopping, doctor's appointments and so forth, on that day. Until Agnes came I also had my household help that day, so that I could briefly leave the kids. But with the approach of my return to work, as well as the many activities to which I needed to drive the children, a second car seemed in order. Our neighbors, the Curchaks, were selling their second car, and we purchased it for the princely sum of seventy-five dollars. It was a ten year old Dodge, and the children christened it Greenie, in deference to its paint color. During the three years we owned it, it did yeoman duty and contributed substantially to our convenience. In those three years, the only money we put into it was to buy a heavy-duty battery, as the car was no longer being pampered by living in a garage. But all good things come to an end, and Greenie was no exception. Her floor-boards rusted through, so that after a rain the front-seat passenger would find water splashing around his ankles. The motor was going strong, but the body of the car was quite disreputable. Sam and I decided to spring for a station wagon, and Greenie went up for sale. It was thirteen years old; we felt we had either to sell it or give it a Bar Mitzvah! The children were aghast; how could we do such a thing? I explained that she was a 1955 model. Sherry blanched. "So am I," she said.

The car sold for fifty dollars – a net loss of twenty-five dollars in three years. Even my super-salesman husband couldn't complain about that.

Uncle Sam Leinwand came with us when we went hunting for a station wagon, while Aunt Mollie stayed with the children. Uncle Sam was a taxi driver, and his income was quite limited, so it was interesting that, when we were at the showroom, Sam and I went to the used car portion while Uncle Sam headed for the new cars. We found a one year old

Chevy wagon that cost $3,000, which was exactly what we had to spend. When we showed it to Uncle Sam, though, he insisted that he had found a much better buy for us – a brand new wagon for only $4,000. We explained that we had only $3,000 available – and he said, "So what? You can finance it." It was hard to convince him that we did not spend money which we didn't have – but our "new" used car served us well for many years.

One of the first major trips we took with that station wagon was camping our way across the country. I was working for a school system at the time, hence had the whole summer off, and Sherry had her newly-minted driver's license. Sam had just four weeks of vacation, so we decided that I would start out with the children. With Sherry spelling me on the driving, we could get halfway there by the time Sam flew out to join us for what we saw as the more interesting portion of the trip. Mark did not like long car trips and wanted to stay at home alone. He was sixteen, and Sam and I would not permit this. However, I offered him choices. He could stay with my parents in the city, he could find some sort of live-in job with at least minimal supervision, or he could find a camp which he could attend during the weeks we were to be away. He had been to camp once when he was ten, but unlike his sisters, he didn't care for it and didn't go again. Now, however, he found himself a music camp in Oneonta, NY which just fit our time requirements, and he had a really terrific experience. Some of the people he met there made him newly aware of the advantages of the city, and probably helped prepare him for a summer internship there at a later time.

As Sam was not much interested in swimming or water sports – he hadn't learned to swim until after we were married and my father taught him – the girls and I made a point of using any available waterside camp grounds while he was not with us. We made camp early enough to swim and canoe, and on one occasion were even able to make camp on an island. We were in the Badlands of South Dakota when Sam flew out to join us a week later. We learned that his colleagues had been shocked! *shocked*! to learn that he had "let" his wife and daughters go off camping by themselves.

I suppose we should have expected it. When I had my first carpel tunnel surgery, an outpatient affair, I asked the doctor if I would be able to drive myself home. As I was having a local rather than a general anesthetic, he agreed that I could. So, of course, I told Sam to go to work as usual. When Sam's co-workers heard that he had not been at my side for the surgery, however, they made him feel so guilty that when I had the other wrist done a year or so later, he insisted on staying home from work and, quite unnecessarily, driving me to and from the hospital.

Camping gave us an inexpensive way to see the immediate world, and we used our pop-up tent-trailer to take us to Canada for Expo 67. Agnes, of course, was with us. The camp ground turned out to be no more than a farmer's field, with hastily-constructed facilities. Unfortunately there was an outbreak of stomach flu at that time, and everyone was vomiting. That was the first of many times when I have seen women take over the men's toilets, refusing to stand in line unnecessarily. As our family succumbed, I had to scatter them around, some sleeping in the car to avoid too close contact. I've always had good disease resistance and was the only healthy one in the crowd. But that was a mixed blessing; you can guess who found herself washing vomit from several sleeping bags - by hand.

CHAPTER XVII: AND THE CHILDREN GREW....

During this time, of course, the children were attending school (where they all did well) and getting involved in a variety of extra-curricular activities. Girl Scouts, Cub Scouts, Sunday School, Band and Chorus, Little League – we lived through them all. I must admit that I was glad when Mark decided not to continue in Little League, though I swear I never discouraged him. But I always attended anything in which my children were involved, and I really had no interest in watching sports. Although I worked three days a week, I was usually able to reorganize my schedule so that I could get to any school performance that involved one of my children. It always intrigued me that so many stay-at-home mothers were not able to do the same.

The children were all interested in dramatics. In fact, Mark's second-grade stint as the wolf in Little Red Riding Hood marked a change in his personality. He had always been rather a shy little boy, but the face-concealing wolf head made him invisible to the audience, and apparently gave him courage. From behind the wolf mask he was able to speak out, and I mark that as the time his shyness began to evaporate. Taking our neighbor, Little Red Riding Hood, home from rehearsal gave me an opportunity to teach him an adult responsibility as well; it was after dark when we dropped her off, and I recall instructing Mark to escort her to the door and wait until she was admitted.

Robin's big part was as the mother rabbit in "The Little Rabbit Who Wanted Red Wings." She had a single two-sentence line – "Wishing, wishing; always wishing. I'm going down to Mr. McGregor's garden!" – which she practiced endlessly. Should she emphasize the first wishing or the second? Or, perhaps, the 'I'm'? Should she sound enthusiastic or bored? Should the end of the line go down or up? The whole family was relieved when the play was finally enacted, and the home rehearsals could be laid to rest.

I had been responsible for providing Robin's costume and made a footed, white flannel rabbit outfit, which could also serve as pajamas. We later got tiger pj's for Mark and some animal – I've forgotten which – for Sherry. Some evenings it looked as though we had quite a menagerie.

Both Sherry and Mark continued their dramatic endeavors in high school, in addition to singing in both chorus and musical plays. Each had major parts in various productions, to their great delight. Sherry was in New Jersey's All-State Chorus, and Mark was both in that and, later, in All-Eastern Chorus. Music continues to be a source of great pleasure to them both. Mark, and briefly Robin, also played instruments in the high school band, leading to an amusing side-note. Our band was selected to go to Washington for a major event, and Mark – as unenthusiastic at early rising as his father – was up at six, preparing for their early departure. When he came down for breakfast, he reported having watched the sunrise while dressing. "It was really neat," he said – "just like a sunset played backwards!"

It is interesting how one's values get tested in almost any issue that arises. I once received a call from a mother regarding the high school band, in which both Mark and Robin played. She wanted me to come to a school board meeting to help convince the Board that the band needed new uniforms. There was nothing the matter with the old ones – but wouldn't the kids look great if they were replaced? I told her I'd be glad to come, but I would speak against that expenditure;

the present uniforms were perfectly usable, and we were, as always, struggling to get more money for books and academic programs.

I cannot leave this time period without speaking of Mark's Bar Mitzvah. Having recently attended my grandson's Bar Mitzvah, I find recollections of my son's flooding back to me. Like Sol's, Mark's was set for a holiday weekend, so that out-of-town family and friends could attend. We scheduled it for Fourth of July weekend, setting it for Monday so that the more Orthodox members of both our families, who did not travel on Shabbat, would be able to attend. A Bar Mitzvah can take place at any service where there is reading from the Torah, and that includes Mondays and Thursdays as well as Saturdays. Our temple, Temple Shalom of Cedar Grove, was enlarging its sanctuary, and work was delayed till Tuesday so that we could have our service before construction began.

We had invited the Nicoloffs and the Baylisses – Peggy's family with six children, and Ella's family with five – to stay at our house for the weekend, to save them the cost of hotels. Including our own family, there were 20 people scheduled to sleep over, and we set up the basement as a dormitory for nine girls, with the few boys sharing Mark's room. Sherry asked if her dear friend from up the hill, Lisa, could sleep over as well; she had no cousins, and this would be a rare treat. I said that Lisa was always welcome, but we had only three bathrooms. Sherry assured me that if Lisa needed the bathroom, she could run up the hill, and the deal was struck. So we had ten girls sleeping in the basement, and I don't remember any line-ups at the facilities. Sam had hung a rod for the girls' dresses, the iron lived in the basement anyway, and our twenty-one guest night was a success.

Mark did a beautiful job, and everyone was quite impressed.

My very religious Aunt Mollie, who admitted to having thought poorly of Reform Judaism, was gracious enough to tell me that our service was beautiful and had made her rethink her prejudice.

We had hoped to have the party in our back yard, but by the time we added up the cost of hiring a Kosher caterer and renting chairs and a tent (not only in case of rain, but because of the possibility of intense heat and sun) it ran to more than using a Kosher catering hall, so we opted for the latter. We followed it up with a reception at home that evening, with all the neighbors in attendance.

CHAPTER XVIII: TRAVEL

Sam and I were both interested in travel, and around our tenth anniversary we began the custom of taking a trip every five years. Though Sam enjoyed our camping trips with the children, he felt the need for some time away from the family. Also, with our major savings going towards college, we really couldn't have afforded trips abroad for all five of us.

Oddly enough, that first trip – three days each way by boat to Nassau, with a week spent on that island – was the focus of perhaps the most painful time in our whole relationship. Sam was having a hard time accepting that he was thirty-nine – "I'm as old as Jack Benny," he would say – and felt the need to somehow reward himself for his long hours and hard work by something of a luxury vacation. I felt – and still feel – that Robin was too young for her parents to leave her for two weeks, even with her well-loved grandparents. Though he later denied it, I clearly recall Sam's saying he would go without me, if necessary. I felt completely torn between what I saw as the needs of my child and the needs of my husband. As icing on the cake, I have always done poorly in hot weather, and the thought of a Nassau holiday was far from appealing. It is surely ironic that I remember that first vacation abroad as the low point in our fifty years of marriage.

However, that did not deter us from planning future trips, and each was more delightful that the other. At our fifteenth anniversary we took a three week trip called European Capitals, sponsored by National Council of Jewish Women. They run fantastic trips, first class all the way, and we enjoyed time in Paris, Rome, London, Switzerland, and Amsterdam. Agnes was with the children, and my Aunt Anna came out to stay with them as well. Of course, we sent cards and letters to the children from every stop we made. I recall sending one from the Eiffel Tower which I signed "Your peregrinating parents," knowing Sherry would look it up in the dictionary. It became something of a joke in our family, as our travels thereafter took us far and wide. Often we took a tour, but sometimes, where language was not a problem, we planned our own itinerary.

In Amsterdam, we met a woman who had been my pen-pal some twenty years earlier. We had been part of a Girl Scout/Girl Guide project, and exchanged letters on a regular basis. She was learning English, which was, of course, the language of our communication. My mother would type a copy of Thea's letter to me, triple spaced, and then retype it underneath with any corrections, including idiomatic suggestions. I would enclose these with my own letters to Thea. We lost contact during the war; my last communication from her had been a postcard, purporting to be for collecting stamps, which I was to send on to other recipients. It was her family's way of letting us know that some of them, at least, were still alive. When Sam and I began to plan our European trip, I found Thea's old pre-war address in Maastricht. Never really expecting to reach her, I wrote to that address and received a response within two weeks. She told me that my letter had reached Maastricht, and the postmaster had telephoned every Tulliken in the phone book until he reached someone who knew her address – it was her father, in fact – and then forwarded the letter to her in Amsterdam. As she put it, "The good old Dutch post office came through!" I tried to visualize the Bronx postmaster doing something similar! In any event, she turned out to be a professional tour guide and attributed part of her language skills to my mother's assistance so many years before.

As celebration of our twentieth anniversary Sam and I spent three weeks in the British Isles, staying at bed-and-breakfasts throughout England and Scotland, as well as spending a couple of days at a London hotel. It was great staying with families in this way; we got something of a feel for the people, instead of being with other Americans at a hotel. In one Scottish home I noticed a guitar, and we swapped Scottish and American folk songs. In another, the woman was a knitter, and we enjoyed sharing our interest in that as well. We got as far north as Inverness and began to understand what was meant by "the midnight sun;" it was light for most of the night. Once we saw the teen-aged son of the family repairing his car in the driveway at about ten-thirty PM – by natural light.

For some months before our twenty-fifth anniversary, I had been squirreling away bits of money without telling Sam. It felt very odd to be hiding something from him, but I wanted to give him a trip to Mexico as a gift. That was where he had wanted to go for our honeymoon, and I felt it was overdue. I had managed to save about $2500. He was astonished and thrilled – but asked if we could go to Israel instead. So we went to Israel. The tour was organized by the Jewish National Fund, and as I was working for a school system at the time, it was during the summer. What a mistake! Due to the heat, I felt sick most of the time. I lay in the back of the bus and often didn't even get out for sightseeing. At one point I actually was running a fever; we were staying at a Kibbutz that night, and I had my first taste of national health care; the doctor would not let me pay for his services. So though I was excited to be in Israel, I can't say I enjoyed the trip. Sam, of course, who never noticed weather, had a really soul-satisfying experience, marred only by my inertia. I might add that, many years later, we went on a Federation 'mission' to Israel. This time it was in November, and we both had a really wonderful experience.

Other trips included three weeks in Alaska, accompanied by Irma and Arnold Bloom; a couple of weeks in Scandinavia, where Molly and Alex Katz were our companions, and a lovely week in Ireland with Judi and Lee. I've mentioned elsewhere our trip to Japan, visiting Peggy and Phil. A five week trip into the depths of Australia fulfilled a lifelong dream of mine, though the flight was so long that we broke it with stops in each direction, at Tahiti in one direction and the Fuji Islands in the other. And when we went to Spain, bringing Robin with us for that trip, we relied on Sam's Spanish rather than joining a tour. Robin has a somewhat olive skin tone, like Sam's; with her oval face and long, dark hair she was often taken for Spanish.

Another major destination was China. Sam had spent three years with Naval Intelligence during the war, almost all of it in China. A natural linguist, he had learned enough Mandarin Chinese to communicate pretty well by the time he was discharged. He got some Berlitz language CD's and regained some of his ability in Chinese before we started on our five week trip. He was eager to revisit some of the places he had been before and found the changes in the country amazing. But one thing had not changed – the Chinese penchant for bargaining. Of course, that was right up Sam's alley, and he had a great time negotiating at markets in a cross between Chinese and English, while people stood around cheering, sometimes for the vendor and sometimes for Sam. I have a beautiful double-horse carved chop (Chinese name stamp) which Sam purchased for me for the price of five dollars, a can of tuna fish and a can of bug spray.

CHAPTER XIX: COMMUNITY

Sam and I were, as always, heavily involved in various community activities. Our town was fairly conservative, and I think our outspoken liberal politics made us appear as the local radicals. A friend of mine once told me that she had suggested my name for corresponding secretary for the PTA, but the nomination was not accepted; "The Zitters are controversial figures in this town!" was the response of the nominating committee's chair. (What damage I might have done as corresponding secretary escapes me, but I never got the opportunity to find out.) But we had friends who shared our views, and who often worked with us on various projects. The Goodmans were high on that list. We met them through our Temple, and as Jerry and Sam both worked in Jersey City, they sometimes drove to work together. Helene, like Sam, was an avid tennis player. And both of the Goodmans were enthusiastic and competent gardeners. They had a large property planted primarily with azaleas, but also with many other shrubs and flowers. Jerry had at one time been president of the American Rhododendron Society, and both of them were exceptionally knowledgeable about gardening. I remember Jerry digging up a small stand of white birch to give us, and my garden was graced with more than one shrub presented to us by the Goodmans. Helene was also a political activist, and I loved having her at my side at some of our great marches on Washington. She has served on several community boards and committees, and is probably the most politically and socially active of my friends. Time and distance have not diminished our friendship

There have been a few major themes in my life – areas and philosophies into which I have put much of my time and energy. As I've said, the two which stand out most strongly are civil rights and women's rights, particularly reproductive rights.

The fifties and sixties saw tremendous emphasis on and progress in the civil rights areas – though never, of course, quite enough. Both through ADA and in our own community, Sam and I were very much involved. Cedar Grove was an all-white town, and I was determined to change that. I advertised a meeting to kick off a Fair Housing Committee, and my living-room filled with a variety of interested citizens, from the mayor on down. One of my friends, Joan Lynn, was a tall, elegant blond – very WASPish looking. We used her as our 'white tester'; when a black family was turned down for a rental or told that a house was sold, we sent her to see if she got the same response. If not, we had documentation that could be brought to court. It never went that far; the mere fact that it could be done seemed to serve our purpose. While it was gratifying to see how many people were eager to help, it was also disheartening to find so many who were opposed to allowing black families the simple right to live where they chose.

We kicked off the project when my dear friend Helen, two houses away, had to move to Boston. Through membership in CORE (Congress of Racial Equality), I had become acquainted with a racially mixed couple, an American Negro (as we then called them) and a 1st generation Japanese-American. They bought Helen's house, and we became quite friendly. In fact, when they had children, my daughters used to baby-sit for them. You will understand what a radical thing the Fair Housing Committee was to some people when I tell you that we later learned from another black resident that he had sat up all night, his first night in Cedar Grove, with a shotgun, ready to defend his family in case of a cross-burning.

Those were days in which the Ku Klux Klan was still active in parts of the country, and an all-out effort was under way to integrate public schools nationally. There were schools being set up for Negro children in Mississippi whose parents did not want to send them to the segregated public schools. A call went out for donated books; my older daughter, Sherry, got a large carton on which she painted the words, "BOOKS FOR MISSISSIPPI NEGRO CHILDREN!" Then she made an impassioned plea to her sixth-grade class, explaining the need and asking for books. At the end of the week, there were only three books in the carton. Outraged, Sherry made another blistering speech – which, as I recall, netted us a few more books.

Those were also the days when the great marches on Washington were taking place: for civil rights, for school integration, for women's rights and reproductive choice - and Sam and I were almost always there. We took our nephew, Wes, with us on his very first march. Later we were accompanied by his then-fiancée (now his wife) Laurie, and it pleases me to realize that, several decades later, we were in the company of his daughter Emily on her first march as well. On that latter occasion, Emily was seven and I was seventy-eight. Sam had already died, and Sherry was my companion. Emily and I both were sagging by mid-afternoon, and Sherry and I agreed that next time we would bring a wheelchair. I could use it as a walker when marching, and she could push me when I needed to sit down.

My pro-choice activities were far from limited to marching, however. I wrote fundraising letters for Planned Parenthood, wrote Letters to the Editor (some of which were actually published) and at a later date served as a volunteer Pregnancy Options Counselor at Planned Parenthood in Trenton. But my major activity came when I retired from working in the school system and continued only with my half-time private practice. I had been a board member of NJ Right To Choose, and as I now had more time available, I began to speak in high schools and some colleges, as well as at college health fairs, on behalf of pro-choice issues. I shortly became president of that organization, a position I retained for the next twenty years.

I also had occasion to speak with adult groups, whether PTA, church or synagogue, or other organizations. On various occasions I represented RCAR (The Religious Coalition for Reproductive Choice) as well as, of course, Planned Parenthood. As a representative to Choice, NJ, I also gave testimony at our State Legislature. Some of those presentations are still in my file; I have no current need of them, but I get pleasure each time I come across them.

Have I described my professional activities during all this time? After four years at Overbrook Hospital, I worked for three years at the West Essex Family Service, doing work I loved and receiving supervisory and consultative service from a top-notch clinician, Nancy Shulte. I was involved with both the National Association of Social Workers and the NJ Association of Clinical Social Workers, the latter of which I served for several years as treasurer. I also participated in a leaderless supervisory group comprised of local clinicians, both social workers and psychologists, who wanted to improve our skills. It was also during this time that I took a two year course at the Family Institute of New Jersey, which awarded me certification in Family Therapy. The skills I learned there were enormously helpful in my practice. I also obtained certification in Group Therapy, and though I found less need for those skills, I did quite a bit of parent education and ran educational groups in a variety of settings.

Sam always worked very long hours. He had developed

a pattern when Sherry was small, which he continued throughout the ensuing years; anything which came across his desk at work which could be handled away from the office got tossed into his briefcase. He would come home between six and six-thirty, in time to have dinner with the family. When the children were little, he would try to spend some time with them, helping me with bathing and putting them to bed. After that, he would go to the desk and work, sometimes until midnight. As I worked only three days a week during those years, I tried to spare him what I could in other household chores, so that whatever free time he had could be spent with the children. Considering his long hours, he managed to spend a surprising amount of time with them. I might add that, in that day and age, this was somewhat atypical.

Our sense of family ran deep. Sam was a terrific salesman; he would occasionally travel with a salesman, helping him with difficult sales or helping train him to be more effective on his own. At one point, Lightolier offered Sam a sales district of his own. It might have been tempting; it would almost treble his income. But it would also have meant being away from home an average of three or four nights a week, and we had no trouble turning it down. We were both frugal; we were living comfortably enough on our then-current income, and having Sam home with the family most nights took precedence over whatever additional luxury we could have purchased.

I think I had more familiarity with tools than did Sam at the time of our marriage. My mother had always insisted that all her children learn to do household tasks in a gender-neutral manner – thus Barry learned to cook and sew, and I painted and did minor repairs, as well as the other way around. But when Sam decided to do something, his persistence was amazing, and he soon became a top-notch do-it-yourselfer. We set up a lockable workshop in the basement and acquired a fair number of power and other tools. We also found ways to include the children in these activities, though I think the girls enjoyed them more than did Mark. They also pitched in on the gardening, though again Mark enjoyed this less than did the girls. I remember when he started mowing the lawn at around age twelve. (Sherry had performed that chore for the previous two summers, but developed some allergies which made that a poor choice of job for her.) After a while, Mark told me, "You know, I don't really enjoy mowing the lawn – but I do enjoy the fact that it is such a help to Dad." A couple of years later, a neighbor of ours, Sophie Singman, wanted to hire Mark to mow her lawn. He turned her down, but Robin was eager to take it on. Though a working woman herself, Sophie apparently was a sexist at heart and refused to hire a girl for this job.

It was too bad, for Robin was one of the most self-directed people I have ever known. In that aspect, she reminds me of both my mother and Sam. She had suffered all her academic life by being compared to Sherry and Mark; when a teacher saw her name, she would always give some version of "Oh, you're Sherry and Mark's sister? I just know you'll be a wonderful student!" And though she certainly was, the constant reiteration of that theme infuriated her. When it began to crop up again in high school, coupled with some of the rigidity of the principal and his rules, she had reached her limit; she was ready to drop out of school!

A younger sister myself, I certainly was sympathetic. I told her that leaving school was not an option; however, if she could find a school in the area that she thought would be more to her liking, we would try to arrange for a transfer. She did her research and came up with an alternative school, housed within Montclair High, which seemed right to her. It was three miles away, and Robin was ready to walk or bike the distance, though it was also possible to get there by bus. The out-of-town fee was not high, and she made the transfer.

The difference to her was phenomenal. For the first time, nobody knew her family, and she felt accepted as her own person. A self-starter, she was able to handle the minimal structure with ease, and she got really "turned on" to school, especially literature, as she never had before. She must have been completely responsible in getting herself there and back, for I recall no difficulties of transportation ever arising.

CHAPTER XX: THE KIDS ARE ON THEIR WAY

Our children were always each others' best friends. Though they all had friends of their own ages, and many of their activities were dissimilar, it was a joy to me to see how they looked out for one another and were there with support and comfort when needed. Both girls were particularly protective of Mark, and it showed up in amusing ways. When they were little, if someone offered Robin a cookie, her other hand would come up as she asked, "And one for Mark?" They even ganged up to protect him from me. The children had always had household responsibilities, but when Mark was around seven or eight, I decided that they were quite old enough to make their beds on a more regular basis. I didn't demand it on school days, but expected it on weekends and holidays before they could go out to play. With the girls, this was no problem, but Mark resisted. When he asked if he could go out, I would ask, "Is your bed made?" The answer was no, and I assured him he could go out as soon as this was done. For two weekends, he remained indoors. I didn't nag; I just stuck to my guns. Then one day his answer was yes! I said, "Good for you, Mark; you made your bed!" My honest little son explained that he hadn't made it; Sherry and Robin had taken pity on him and made it for him. When I spoke to them about it, they were indignant; what did I care who made it, as long as it got made? I told them that I cared very much; I was not raising helpless people, and we each had to be responsible for our own chores.

Mark showed early signs of the entrepreneur which he would eventually become. At one point, he went into the car-washing business with Robin and a friend from the next block, Joe Noto. Joe was a husky lad a year older than Mark, and

Robin was always gung-ho for any work. I supplied them with soap and rags, and they were off. When I came out to see how they were doing, I found Robin and Joe up to their elbows in soapy water, while Mark, clean and dry, was handling the money and dealing with customers.

I might mention that Joe, for whom English was a second language, was a bit slower academically than the other children in the neighborhood, and his parents were eager to improve his schoolwork. My children came home one day to tell me that Joe would get five dollars for every 'A' he received on his report card; what would they get? My reply? "My heartiest congratulations!"

Speaking of money, I might mention that we had started the children on allowances as soon as they could add simple sums – around grade one or two. I do not believe in allowances as payment for chores; chores are your portion of the family responsibilities and must be done with no other reward than your knowledge that you are pulling your weight. An allowance, on the other hand, is your share of family income – almost an entitlement. As its purpose is also to teach the child how to handle money, withholding it as punishment makes little sense to me. Also, if chores are paid for, then a child could decide he didn't need the money and he wouldn't do the chores. That logic didn't work in our family.

The allowance started at fifteen cents a week, and there were three parts to it. A nickel was for long-term saving (you might want to buy something which cost more than one or two weeks' worth of allowance) – a nickel for spending, and a nickel for charity. The children could each chose a favorite charity, which often varied from time to time. I also tried to convey some of my beliefs about use of money. First was that, no matter how little you had, there was always someone even more needy, so that a portion of any income should be allocated for giving. Secondly, if you don't have enough, there are really only two possible options: earn more or spend less. Sherry was always one who would spend less; Mark would try to earn more. And Robin might well do both. It is with pride that I can say that, at one time or another, each of my children has come to me to thank me for teaching him or her how to handle money.

That reminds me of another basic bit of my child-rearing philosophy. It relates to structure, which I see as the supporting framework on which personality and character are built. To me, there is a great difference between discipline and punishment. Discipline sets up a pattern, a structure, which helps a child know what is expected, when it must be done, and that there are natural consequences to not doing it. An example: Sam was much tidier than I by nature and did not feel relaxed when there was too much clutter. The children knew that the front hall had to be cleared of all extraneous items – school books, jackets, mail, etc. – before Daddy came home. Dinner did not get served until the front hall was clear. It was never "because you didn't pick up your stuff, you can't watch television," but rather, "As soon as the front hall is picked up, we can have dinner." The first would be punishment – ie, revenge for wrongdoing. The latter I see as discipline. Similarly, it was never "Because you didn't finish your homework, you can't watch TV (or whatever the goal of the moment might be) but rather, "As soon as you finish your homework, you may do…." whatever it was. A favorite program might occasionally be missed, but they knew they had the chance to work their way toward whatever was their goal. I might add that TV was limited so closely that none of my three children has grown up to be a TV addict. There was a point at which I was probably the only mother in America with three adult children, living separately, none of whom owned a television set.

I've been describing how hard Robin worked, and what energy she poured into everything. But she was less easy-going than the others and often used that same energy to oppose me. I had to think very fast sometimes, as she tried to box me into a corner. Here are a few examples from when she was around nine or ten. "Mommy, do I have to go to college?" I told her that I thought she would want to go, but no, it was not something she had to do. "Well, if I don't, what will you do with the money you're saving for me?" I said that Daddy and I might take a trip around the world with it. "You won't give it to me?" No, I explained; we were saving that money for college, because it was something important that we wanted to give to her. But for luxuries like trips, she would have to save just as we did. Hmm.

Again, a question: "When I'm grown-up, can I live here?" At that particular moment, the idea did not appeal to me at all (I hasten to add that I have since changed my mind most dramatically) but I answered, "Do you mean when you are through school and working?" Yes, that was what she meant. "Well," I told her," I don't think you'll want to, but if you like, of course you can live here. You'd pay room and board, of course…." "What is that?"

"That's the money you pay for the food you eat and the room where you sleep." Robin was genuinely shocked! "You'd charge your own child for sleeping in her own bed?" "Oh, no, Robin," I assured her. "Not when you're a child. Then we take care of you, of course. But we were talking about when you are all grown up. One of the ways you know you're grown up is that you take care of yourself."

"Well," declared Robin, "there's no point in living here then, is there!"

Another time the question was, "Would you let me marry someone who wasn't Jewish?" – clearly expecting me to say no, so she could declare that I couldn't stop her. But I said, "Robin, I wouldn't *let* you marry anybody. If you need my permission, then you aren't mature enough to get married." There wasn't much of anywhere she could go with that one!

CHAPTER XXI: MORE ABOUT FAMILY

Throughout our marriage, Sam and I have had an astonishingly large number of elderly relatives to keep track of. Sam's father was one of six siblings, but of those six, Pop was the only one who had children – and of those children, we were the only ones able to look after the family. Itch lived in California, Bob in Illinois, and both of their wives were antagonistic toward their in-laws. Sol, wheelchair-bound, shared care of Mom with their Uncle Al, all three continuing to live together in Miami Beach after Pop's death. We were fortunate that we never needed to support these aunts and uncles financially, but a good deal of our time was spent looking after them, traveling to the other end of Brooklyn or down to Florida. My sister, subsequent to a stroke, also ended up in a nursing home for the last several years of her life, and I visited her weekly all during that time. And my mother needed pretty much full-time care during the last year of her life.

The years seemed to fly by, and our children continued to grow and change and develop. I cannot possibly recall all the funny and delightful things which occurred during that time, but a few family stories do come to mind. Activities included music lessons, school dramatics, singing in chorus (state-wide and national as well as local), playing in the school band, Girl Scouts, Cub Scouts, and other activities too numerous to mention, much less to recall. I had a huge calendar on the wall on which I tried to keep track of everyone's comings and goings. Not only would I be providing a lot of the transportation, but I also tried to adjust dinner so that we usually could all eat together. As I've mentioned, Sam had early developed a pattern of getting home for dinner with the family, even though he often had to stay up till midnight to complete his work, and that time together was precious to us all. The children often had guests for dinner, and I later learned that some of them were fascinated by our lively conversation. Apparently, in some homes politics and philosophy are not regularly served up with dinner.

When the family was alone for dinner, I would sometimes read an item out loud with an eye to stimulating some thinking or discussion. Once I read about a child who had been assigned to write about some kind – any kind – of family. She chose to write about a poor family. "The family was very poor," she wrote. "The father was poor. The mother was poor. The little girl was poor. Even the chauffeur was poor." We all laughed except for six-year-old Robin, who said, "I don't think it's funny. It's not funny to be poor." Sherry explained kindly, "If they were so poor, they wouldn't have a chauffeur." I said, "If they were so poor, they wouldn't have a car." Startled, my ten-year-old child of the suburbs asked, "Not even one?"

It must have been somewhere around that time when, on our anniversary, I found a card at my place at table. The front showed a round little pink housewife with a golden halo – and the words said, "It's our anniversary, and you've been a *good* wife." Then inside, it added, "Guess I'll keep you another year!" I laughed, then passed it around the table for the children to see. Sherry read it, also laughed, and said "Yes, Daddy, I think you *should* keep her another year." Sam asked, "And what will I do with her after that7?" Sherry responded, "I think you should keep her another two years." Sam asked, "And what will I do with here after that?" Said Sherry, "I think you should keep her another *five* years." And Sam asked, "And what will I do with her after that?" Sherry declared, "I think you should keep her another *ten* years!" And Sam asked, "And what should I do with her after that?" Going all out, Sherry asserted, "I think you should keep her another

TWENTY years!" And Sam asked, "And what should I do with her after that?" Ten year old Sherry, blushing, admitted "I figured you'd both be dead by then!"

The children shared our liberal views, and Sherry in particular became an early activist. Like Sam and me, she wrote Letters to the Editor and involved herself in working for various causes. I shall reproduce here a letter which we jointly sent to the Times, though I do not have the article which prompted it.

16 Reservoir Place
Cedar Grove, NJ 07009
February 8, 1983

To the Editor
The New York Times

We highly commend New York Education Commissioner Gordo M. Ambach for his enlightened proposal that children begin school at age four and graduate following 11th grade. The economic logic behind the idea seems indisputable: Although the same number of years would be spent in school, the saving on school lunch programs would be substantial! Twelfth graders notoriously eat more than do four year olds.

There is precedence on which to base this assumption that legislation can speed the development of children. After all, if the Family Protection Act can legislate adolescent chastity on a national basis, why cannot New York State legislate reading readiness at the age of four?

In the further interest of efficiency, how about age three?

Sarai G. Zitter. M.S.W.
Sherry M. Zitter
Cedar Grove, N.J.

Sherry also was Editor-in-Chief of her high school newspaper at the time of the famous Roe v. Wade decision. Reproductive rights had been all over the newspapers, and Sherry and her friend Dennis wrote opposing editorials, she in favor of freedom of choice and he opposed to it. The principal refused to let them be printed, on the grounds that high school students shouldn't be thinking about such things. Sherry then wrote an editorial about freedom of the press, which the principal also banned. She contacted the ACLU, which was interested but, overloaded with cases, they moved too slowly; Sherry had graduated (as Salutatorian) before they were able to be of assistance. I have always wished that case could have been carried through to completion.

I had been dubious about Sherry's accepting that editorship. She was involved with numerous activities, and I had always worked with her to help her keep from falling into the trap of overloading. But I realized that she would be going off to college, where she would have to self-regulate her work load. If she were going to fall on her face, better it be while she was still at home and we could help her pick up the pieces. So, though we discussed our concerns with her, we left the decision in her hands.

The children all chipped in on chores, of course, but I usually prepared and served dinner. My luxury, started when Sherry was barely old enough to carry a cup, was remaining at the table after dinner and having my coffee served to me. She did this all the way through high school, and when she went off to college Mark took over, only to be replaced in turn by Robin. When Robin was getting ready to leave for college, I asked woefully, "But who will bring me my coffee?" Sam said nobly, "I will!" Though he was more than willing, it didn't happen too often; as a much faster eater than he, I found it difficult to wait. But as always, his heart was in the right place.

I might mention that the children all had to take occasional turns at preparing a meal. They could also get out of helping with the dishes by cooking dinner instead; then I would assume their clean-up detail. In this way, they all became competent cooks. Normally they took turns doing the dishes, usually two of them at a time. Mark managed to convince the girls that he was doing his share if they did the dishes and he entertained them by playing his accordion. Again I intervened, requiring that we each do our own chores.

We have often chuckled about an incident related to chores and cooking. I was having elective surgery on my ear – it had been suggested that it might be possible to restore some of the hearing to my deaf ear – and would be in the hospital for four days. That worked out well – I assigned Sam and the children each to a night's dinner preparation and made myself available to help them work out details of their plans. Of course, they visited me each evening, and I was given a glowing report of what they had for dinner. Sam cheated – he took them out to a restaurant – but the kids loved it. When it was Mark's turn, he announced proudly, "I served pot roast tonight!" Startled, the woman in the next bed turned over and asked, "Homemade pot roast?" Mark, who had never heard of any other kind, said "Of course." I did not think it necessary to explain that I had cooked the pot roast, sliced it and frozen it in its gravy; Mark had defrosted and heated it. This was the norm in our house, as we had a big freezer. Mark had added vegetables, dessert, etc. – in other words, had turned out a fine meal. But my room-mate was mightily impressed with my fifteen year old chef.

I suppose it is inevitable that parents sometimes embarrass their children. Robin, though in many ways an iconoclast, was particularly sensitive to our doing anything that her friends' parents didn't do. Sam and I enjoyed square dancing, and were active in a Modern Western Square Dance Club, complete with fancy costumes. One night we told the children that our club would be doing a demo at the nearby mall, and we would participate. Robin asked anxiously, "When?" We told her it would be that Wednesday, and she heaved a dramatic sigh of relief, exclaiming, "Thank goodness! None of my friends shops on a Wednesday!"

CHAPTER XXII: THE EMPTYING NEST

College days were approaching for Sherry, and a lot of dinner-table conversation revolved around college choices, expenses and plans. Sam and I had started a college fund for each child right after birth and continued to fund them through the leanest of years. I had originally started Sherry's fund with $15 a month, and then did the same for Mark. When Robin was born, we literally did not have another $15 leeway in our budget, so we reduced the other two to $10 a month and started Robin's at that level. It was a proud day when, a few years later, I was able to up them all to $25 monthly. Of course, when I went back to work, we were able to save more than we had before, but now with college on the horizon, I felt that full-time work was in order. Robin heard all this discussion and suggested that perhaps she should get an after-school job to help toward her own college expenses. I pointed out that she was already helping in that department; the fact that she functioned so well at home, and was so responsible with her chores, helped make it possible for me to work – and while I could earn so much more at my age than she could at twelve, an hour of her work at home was absolutely equivalent to an hour of mine! It was typical of Robin to be ready to work. Whatever task she assigned herself, she followed through to its conclusion with energy and persistence. Neither Sam nor I ever demanded that our children get top grades, only that they do their best. I am sure that many people must have thought we put pressure on Robin, because she drove herself so hard, pouring her whole heart into each assignment. Mark, though he worked hard at what interested him, could be more lackadaisical at times, and I remember one evening when I was standing between their rooms, giving very different advice to each. To Mark I said, "Don't try to impress me with that A. You know and I know that you put very little effort into that assignment." – and then saying to Robin, "Relax; not everything is worth one hundred and one percent of your effort."

One more thing I must mention regarding college costs. At one point during our discussions, Sherry said, "Don't worry. If something happens to you and Dad, I'll see to it that Robin gets to college." Of course, she had no idea of what a vast commitment that would have entailed, but I was enormously touched.

Another college comment: Sherry decided on her own that, though Sam and I were financing her college, she should be making a contribution to it as well. She had some baby-sitting money saved (the rule always had been that a portion of any income went to savings, and another portion to charity) and now she could also work during the summers. She paid for her own incidental expenses at college, and in so doing set a pattern which the others followed as well.

For some reason, this reminds me of an incident from my own youth. College was under discussion, and Mother, no fan of housework, said, "I'd scrub floors if necessary, to see that you could get to college." I laughed. "I can just see you scrubbing floors," I said. Mother fixed me with a stern eye, and what she said I've never forgotten. "There is no job which it is beneath me to do," she declared. "The only thing which is beneath me is to do less than my best!" Pow!

As one way of helping to defray college costs, we began to rent the children's unused bedrooms to students from Montclair College, just a few blocks away. There was a shortage of dormitory space, and an appeal had been made to neighbors to make space available. Our first renter was a music major, a young cellist named Karen Hoogerhyde; she stayed with us not only for her junior and senior years of college, but for two years after that. She really felt like part of the family. Sherry even noticed a Girl Scout uniform moving in with her. Karen came to us just after Agnes got married, and Agnes's downstairs room became hers. Later, as the children went off to college, we let their rooms help pay for their expenses. As the school years were similar, the rooms were again available for our children when they came home.

As we added these others to our household, I used our initial interview to clarify rules and mutual expectations. I let them know that visitors were welcome, but their boyfriends were not welcome to spend the night. We were a non-smoking family, and drugs, including marijuana, were not acceptable in the house. They were welcome to use the kitchen, except between 5:30 and 7:30, when it was reserved for my family. They could use the laundry equipment. No noise after ten P.M. I only had one or two people who looked at the rooms and decided against them, and I suspect that my clarity about standards was the reason. And that was exactly why I was so specific. In all our years of renting rooms, I don't recall a single real problem.

CHAPTER XXIII: AND YET MORE FAMILY

When Sam and I moved to Cedar Grove, he said it would be our first five-year house. We expanded and altered it in several ways, having at one time as many as seven bedrooms, but it was thirty-nine years before we moved to Greenbriar. Located in Monroe Township, NJ, Greenbriar is what they call an Active Adult Community, and we bought what we expected would be our last home. After so many years in a split-level house, we were glad to move into what was essentially an expanded ranch. With two bedrooms, two baths and a large den on the main floor, we could pretty much live there without ever climbing stairs, while enjoying the luxury of two guest rooms and a bath upstairs. Thus we had room for all the kids when they came, as well as the assortment of nephews, nieces, cousins and friends who visited from time to time.

We were also blessed with several grandnieces of whom we made very good use. After all, as I pointed out to my grandfather-ready husband, with grandchildren you get to take them places, buy them things, have fun with them – and we did all these things with our grandnieces. Once, when Rachel was only four, my niece Ruthie and her husband Dave wanted to send her down to visit with Bobby and Barry, her grandparents. I was going from their house to the Boston area, so I delivered Rachel to Sherry, who was heading for New Jersey – a convoluted trip, but giving us each a chance for a visit. To break up the long drive I brought my tent, and Rachel and I stopped at a camp ground along the way. The man checking us in saw that there was no man in our party and asked, "Who is going to help you set up the tent?" "She is," I responded, pointing to four-year-old Rachel, who promptly put her hands on her hips and declared, "I am!" Half an hour later that same man drove up to help us out; I think he was rather startled to see that we had our camp all set up and were ready to take a hike around the area.

When Becky was nine, my niece Ruthie was unable to get to Girl Scout Camp for a mothers' weekend, so I was invited as a substitute. We went canoeing, sang around the campfire, and did all the things I remembered from my own Girl Scout Camp days. Becky appreciated my coming – but oh, how I appreciated the opportunity to be there with her.

Our visit to Disneyland with Rachel and Becky was prior to that time – perhaps the year before - but they were about twelve and eight respectively. We rented a condo for the week as a less expensive alternative to hotel rooms, and ate breakfasts and some of our dinners in the apartment. At our first dinner in, Sam automatically cleared the table. The next night, I suggested that we did not want Uncle Sam to do all the clearing up, so I'd like Becky to clear the table and Rachel to wash the dishes; I would put things away. Rachel looked at me blankly and said, "I don't know how to wash dishes!" Knowing her mother, I very much doubted that, but I said, "Aren't you lucky! You have here one of the best teachers in the world on how to wash dishes!" I don't think she suffered too much.

Another treat with Becky was an Intergenerational Elder Hostel at Kent College in Maine. Accompanied by my new sister-in-law Addie (Bobbie had died some years earlier) and her nine year old grandson Craig, we flew to Boston and then boarded a tiny 8-seater plane for the college. The theme of the week was science and technology, and we enjoyed learning math tricks and computer skills as well as performing some fascinating physics experiments.

Julia, Wes's daughter by his first marriage, had her first public outing to my 60th birthday party, when she was precisely three weeks old. As she lived only part-time with Wes, we saw less of her than we did of her cousins, but relationships were always close and loving. It is a pleasure to have her living near me at present. Julia's middle name, Rose, is for my mother (as is my granddaughter Tessa's) – and Mother would have been proud of the lovely young women who bear her name.

Emily, Wes's younger daughter, is just a little older than Sol and thus is almost like one of my grandchildren. Being so near in age, they love being together, and seem destined to have the kind of cousin relationships that their parents and grandparents enjoyed. Emily has been a dog-lover almost from birth; at present, she is learning to race sled dogs. Once, when I was visiting at her home, I was finishing up a sweater which I had knitted for Sol. It had an elephant's face and trunk knitted into the front, its rear end and tail in the back. (I had once knitted a similar sweater for four-year-old Becky; she still had it in her closet when she packed for college.) Seven year old Emily examined the sweater and said, "Of course, Aunt Sis, you know that if you make one for me, it would have to have a doggie on it." I had my marching orders and immediately searched out and knit a sweater with a doggie on it.

We didn't see as much as we would have liked of our West Coast grand-nieces, but did get to California for occasional visits. We took them to playgrounds and amusement parks and got great satisfaction from our continuing relationship. As each girl reached Bat Mitzvah age, our gift was a trip to New Jersey with a week spent sightseeing and going to theatre in New York City – for each, her first trip to the East Coast.

To my great joy, it has turned out to be a two-way street. As adults, both girls have maintained their closeness, first to Sam and me and later to me alone, and have gone out of their ways to visit. When Ashley had a business trip to Philadelphia, she arranged to stay an extra day or two so that I could meet her there, sightsee with her, and bring her home for a brief but delightful visit. When she lived in Florida, she managed a long trip to visit me when I was briefly nearby. And when Heather flew back to Boston from California after finishing college, she took a bus to New York and arranged to spend a day with me there.

I have mentioned our regular saving for our children's college expenses. When our grandnieces were little, we started college funds for each of them as well, and it was a great pleasure to be able to help with those increasingly oppressive costs. Sam and I felt that we had garnered so much richness from our warm, extended families that we delighted in being able to pass some of that on down the line.

One more comment about family: we have been consistently fortunate in our in-laws. Thinking back, I realize that this has been a pattern from the beginning. My mother was very close to Bubby, her mother-in-law, who also was devoted to her daughters- and sons-in-law. Sam and Bobbie were both crazy about my parents, and I have always felt loved and accepted by Sam's entire extended family. As first my cousins, and then my nieces and nephew began to choose mates, they somehow have all blended into a warm and supportive family unit. I could not think of Laurie, for instance, only as my nephew's wife; she is my niece, as Dave (Ruthie's husband) is my nephew. And these newer entrants into the family seem to feel it, too. I recall one of the Jewish holidays when Ruthie was unable to get time off from work, so Dave bundled the girls into the car and drove down without her. Despite a continent between us, Jess and I have managed to stay close and mutually supportive, with respect as well as affection. As for Lee, he 'married in' so long ago that I can hardly believe he wasn't born one of us!

CHAPTER XXIV: OUR LAST HOME TOGETHER

By the time we moved to Greenbriar, the family was quite scattered; Mark was in California, Robin in Connecticut, and Sherry in Massachusetts, while Ruthie was in Ithaca, Wes in New Hampshire, and Arlene, Heather and Ashley still in California – and it was especially important to be able to house them all. And house them we often did, as first the Golomb family Chanukah party and then our huge Seder moved from my parents' home to mine.

Those gatherings were really something special. All my Dad's siblings had lived within a mile or so of each other, and we had grown up with cousins who were halfway to feeling like additional siblings. As the family grew, my mother found creative ways to expand the available space, and everyone managed to crowd in. At one point she had saw horses with boards on top to serve as table extensions, and they reached out into the hall. Lower saw horses served for benches along the walls. But as Mother reached her early seventies, she found it to be too much for her, and several smaller Seders replaced our big one. But after Dad died, my immediate family Seder moved to Cedar Grove, where with relatives and friends I served as many as thirty people on some occasions. As I was working full time, I made good use of the big freezer in the garage. Starting as much as two weeks in advance, I learned that even matzo balls can be frozen.

In choosing our house in Monroe Township, we specifically looked for one which could house these giant dinners, and we couldn't have been happier with what we found. Also, I had the big kitchen that I had always wanted, while Sam had his huge den. Too, I had the pleasure of putting in a new garden, while our community took care of such nuisances as snow removal and lawn care. I didn't grow vegetables here, as I had previously done, as the community used the usual chemicals in their lawn care. In Cedar Grove I had used only organic soil amendments and felt that my home-grown produce was a healthy addition to our diet. But in my new place, I felt that the farmers' markets were a better alternative. Anyway, I was forty years older than I had been at that previous move and had perhaps a tad less physical energy.

We moved to Greenbriar in November of 1995. Sam was due for hip replacement surgery, but we had postponed it until after our move so that he would have no stairs to contend with post-operatively. Thus he was in the hospital for New Year's Eve. We had always had a New Year's Eve party, with some very close friends attending. But this time, Molly and Alex were the only ones who joined us, and we brought champagne to the hospital to see in the New Year. Of course Sam couldn't have any, but the nurses and interns certainly appreciated it.

During that New York hospitalization, as well as the later ones which preceded Sam's death, I had a home away from home with my cousin Ann, who lives on 79th Street on the west side, within bus or walking distance of Sam's various hospitals. It was another example of the blessing my close cousin relationships have been to me all through my life. It meant a great deal to me to come home to a loving, supportive friend, rather than an empty hotel room, during those anxious days.

Sam was recuperating at home the weekend following his surgery and Sherry came down from Boston to visit with him. A massive snow storm accompanied her, and she was snowed in with us for an extra day or two. Greenbriar, as a new community, was not yet equipped for speedy snow removal, so Sherry and I put on Sam's and my cross-country skis and skied around the neighborhood. We later learned that many of our new neighbors were wondering who those crazy women were, out skiing in this weather. Sherry, of course, had helped me shovel out the car, and when the street was cleared, I went food shopping. I asked our next door neighbors, George and Harriette Lewin, if they needed anything. George said they needed bread and milk, but there was no way to get it to them; snow was piled up in front of their doors. No problem: when I got home with the food, I put on my skis again, phoned George to open his garage door, and dropped the bag into his waiting arms. He took a picture of me, several feet above his head on top of the piled snow; he thought nobody would otherwise believe it.

We became good friends with the Lewins, as well as with many others in the community. I was especially close to the Chmiels, and Ellen remains one of my dear friends to this day. Bruno was also my computer guru, and along with the Computer Club can take credit for most of what I know about that wonderful and frustrating instrument. When I moved to Greenbriar, I had only used Sam's computer occasionally as a word-processor; neither of us had any knowledge of the web. But at seventy years old, I could see that this was the wave of the future and I didn't want to be left behind. I joined the Computer Club and found its members to be uniformly generous in sharing their knowledge with us beginners. They ran regular classes, both in Greenbriar and at the library for the larger town community. This knowledge has stood me in good stead as I've taken on the technical work for our community news magazine.

Ellen and I connected on many levels. She is a liberal activist and believes in many of the same organizations and

Sarai G. Zitter

movements which are important to me. She is a seeker, always
asking questions and wanting to understand things more
clearly. And she is a warm and caring friend; despite my later
move, we have kept in close and affectionate contact.

Other activities in this phase of my retirement were the
League of Women Voters and the National Council of Jewish
Women, in the latter of which I had been active for forty
years or so. I also found a wonderful Reform Temple nearby,
Etz Chaim, with the warmest, most supportive congregation
I could have imagined. Although not religious – Sam and I
attended services primarily at the High Holydays, and rarely
on Shabbat – I became quite involved in a variety of Temple
activities. I even sang in the Temple choir – using transliterated
lyrics, as I do not read Hebrew. The depths of my involvement
with Etz Chaim can be imagined when I report that my last
Saturday in town was marked by "Sarai Shabbat," as a tribute
to me.

In any group in which I participated, I always seemed to be
either a member of or the head of the Social Action committee,
and it was no different in these groups. This, of course, put me
in the company of people who believed as I did, so that the work
was also a joy. After a while I was writing a monthly article on
women's health, especially reproductive health, and I adapted
the same information for the League newsletter and that of
National Council. At one point Hadassah – of which I was not
even a member – asked me to conduct a workshop series on
Parenting our Adult Children. Many years earlier I had run a
workshop series for National Council on Grandparenting, and
I realized that I could adapt much of the same material. This
workshop, which I had anticipated would have only a session
or two, became a long running series, terminated only by my
eventual move out of the area. It was a delight for me to be
back doing the work for which I had been trained and which

I so enjoyed.

Although I had left my school job before I was sixty, when Sam retired from Lightolier and we wanted time to travel and do other things together, I had continued with a part-time private practice. When we moved to Greenbriar, however, I decided to give that up as well. I could not expect clients to travel an hour to see me, and at seventy, I was not about to start trying to develop a new set of referral sources. In fact, some of my clients did make the trip for a while, but basically I was retired at the time of the move.

I may not have mentioned my dislike of housework, but even in our leanest financial times I always had some household help. I always loved to cook, never minded dishes or laundry, and enjoyed gardening – but routine cleaning to me was something to avoid. Sam was always far tidier than I, but also disliked cleaning. He could put things away, but leave the counter sticky. I could pick up something to wipe under it, but neglect to put it away. When Sam left his job and I cut back to part-time, he asked me, "Now that we will have so much more time at home, do we still need Hazel?" Hazel was, of course, our cleaner. I looked him straight in the eye and responded, "No, not if you want to take over!" I heard no more about eliminating household help.

In the early days, when Sam was working such long hours and the children were small, I asked very little of him at home. Any free time he had was better spent with the children. And Sam was always very good about pitching in. Also, he was an enthusiastic shopper (though not for food) and ran many of the household errands. But now, with both of us at home full time, I felt ready for a more equitable arrangement. I sat him down and suggested we figure out how to divide our household chores. Sam was surprised and, I think, a little hurt. "Have I ever said 'no' when you've asked me for help?" he wanted to know. I pointed out that this was exactly the point; if I had to ask, then it was *my* job; what I wanted was for some of the jobs to be his, so that I didn't even have to think about them.

To his credit, Sam 'got it', and we decided on laundry as his first major task. I began to explain sorting by fabric and color, what took hot water and what cold, what needed permanent press settings and what couldn't go in the dryer….and Sam, typically, took careful notes. I later saw a single-spaced typed document posted in the laundry room, with all his notes organized. But he had difficulty distinguishing fabrics, and it became more trouble than it was worth. So I did the washing, put selected stuff in the dryer, and left everything for him to fold and put away.

Then he took on doing the dishes. He had often helped with them, but it now became officially his job. He became very possessive of it, too. If, while something was heating on the stove, I began to wash a couple of dishes or a pot, Sam would stop me, saying, "No, that's *my* job!" He may not have enjoyed it, but he certainly was determined to do his share! What a man!

In fact, there was only one aspect of our communication which created problems, and I must admit that this was an issue throughout our marriage. I spoke precisely, and Sam heard approximately! In many cases, this didn't really matter, but sometimes it made a significant difference. My favorite example is when I decided to buy a handsome, modern rocking chair, which meant that I needed a new home for Bubby Shagan's rocker. Robin was happy to accept it, and I asked Sam to glue the rod, which had come loose. He nailed it instead, thus destroying its value as an antique. Even though we didn't intend to sell it, I was still upset. Sam was amazed; hadn't I *asked* him to fix it?

No, I had asked him to *glue* it. I think I can fairly say that some version of this was the only significant communication problem which Sam and I encountered.

CHAPTER XXV: THE FAMILY EXPANDS – AND SHRINKS!

Exactly a year after we moved, we had the delight of welcoming a new member to the family. Mark, who had for some time been looking for just the right wife, finally found her in Jessica, and their November wedding was a joy to us all. The wedding itself gave an idea of the kind of people they are and the kind of home they would be establishing. It was vegetarian, to accommodate both the vegetarians and the kosher-keepers among us, and the facility and caterers were involved in prison rehabilitation endeavors. It was large, traditional and filled with loving family and friends. It felt as though half of the east coast had migrated to California for the occasion.

Jess fit right in – warm, enthusiastic, loving and bright, it was easy to feel I had a new daughter. Sam called her our "designer daughter-in-law," meaning that if he had been asked to design just the right daughter-in-law, Jess is what he would have come up with.

The couple settled in the San Francisco area, where both had been living, but we managed a good many visits back and forth through the ensuing years. Of course, those years were marked with three very significant births – our three wonderful grandchildren. Sol's birth gave us reason to fly right out for his *bris*, and we arrived at the airport expecting to be met by Mark. Instead, we found Mark, Jess, and our new grandson. I said, "I can't believe that you brought a three-day-old infant to the airport," to which Mark replied plaintively, "We didn't want to, but he insisted. He's very strong-willed!"

Sol was followed in seventeen months by Tessa Rose – her middle name was for my mother, as Sol's had been for my father – and a couple of years later, along came Sasha. It is impossible to describe the joy these three little ones brought into our lives. Sam in particular embarked on a whole new career as grandfather. In the past we had teased him that he had "grandfather readiness," and he certainly threw himself into grandfathering with delight.

I have mentioned that our family was big on parties, but I think we hit a new high with my seventieth birthday. You will recall that I have always loved camping. Well, the children planned a weekend camping trip for my birthday party, with my children and grandchildren, my brother and his children and grandchildren, and my beloved cousins Judi and Lee – also campers – with their children and grandchildren as well. There had been some air hijackings, and Jess was hesitant about flying in, but in the end she just couldn't stay away. And Sasha, who was due that coming November, attended *in utero.* We all had such a wonderful time that we decided to do it again, opening it to the rest of the family. It continued as an annual tradition for almost fifteen years and was always the children's favorite weekend. Best of all, it meant that our children got to know their cousins in a way that an occasional afternoon visit never could have achieved. Mark once commented that his children knew their third cousins better than some of his friends knew their first!

Around the time Sasha was born, Mark felt the need to be in New Jersey for business reasons, and Sasha was only a month old when the family moved in with us for a few weeks while they went house-hunting. I put Sasha's crib in my room, while the two older children shared the little bedroom next to mine, so that Jess – still tired from the recent birth – could get more sleep. I had always had a crib in my room when they visited and thoroughly enjoyed those brief periods of again having a baby around. Unfortunately, that was also the time when Sam was dying of leukemia, so there was a dark underside to those days. But for Sam, having the children around was a tonic and gave him tremendous joy.

There recently was a movie entitled "Three Weddings and a Funeral." It reminded me that I have been privileged to officiate at three funerals and a wedding. There is a certain amount of repetition in my funeral remarks, but I am presenting them as they were actually spoken.

The first funeral was that of my friend "Judy B-square," as we used to call her. This was to distinguish her from Judy B, her sister-in-law. I had met both Judy's at farming camp, just before beginning college. That was the same summer that I met Flip, whom you will recall was studying to be a mechanical engineer. Judy Bernstein was also at Cooper, majoring in Chemical Engineering, and we also continued as friends through the years. Judy Bernstein married Nat Baily, Judy B's brother. They lived in Silver Springs, Maryland, just outside of Washington DC, and Sam and I often stayed with them when we were in Washington for ADA conventions. In addition to enjoying the visits, we saved on expensive hotel rates. Once we even camped out for a convention, but found that to be too inconvenient.

Unfortunately, Judy B-square developed a particularly aggressive form of breast cancer. It is significant that her older son also developed cancer at around the same time, as she had been working with chemicals – since found to be highly toxic – during her pregnancy with him. During one of my last visits, Judy declared that she didn't want any kind of religious service; nobody would come to her funeral anyway. I argued with her, assuring her (to her evident surprise) that

I would certainly be there. After her death, Nat asked if I would conduct a service for her, as she specifically did not want a rabbi. As an extra bit of tragedy, her parents were both alive, and Judy died the day before her father's one-hundredth birthday. Guests who had gathered for his birthday celebration attended a funeral instead. I am inserting here the text of what I said on that occasion, resurrected from my notes. That was in 1989, and Judy was, tragically, only 59.

"I'm Sarai Zitter- Sisty, to Judy. Nat asked me to serve as facilitator – and I realized that, outside of blood relatives, I've known Judy longer than anyone else here.

Judy did not want a funeral – any service in a traditional sense – and we are respecting her wishes. But there are so many of us here who cared about Judy. What we'd like to do today is share some of our thoughts, some of our recollections, and in doing that, we'll share our strength and offer one another our support.

Each of you is invited to think about something – perhaps an incident, a shared experience, or just an expression of some thoughts and feelings as you remember Judy. And don't be afraid to recall something humorous; Judy would have liked us to include laughter in our remembrances of her. And then, I invite you to tell us of your recollections or thoughts.

As we are such a large group, and I hope that many of us will have something to say, let me ask that we limit ourselves to just a couple of minutes apiece. If you'd like to speak, just stand up – and please tell us who you are, and how you know Judy.

It is hard to limit myself to two or three minutes; my heart is full, and I could easily go on for an hour or two. Judy and

I met when we were seventeen – picking strawberries and string beans for the war effort. I was attracted by her total love of life, her ability to enjoy things to the fullest. And as our friendship matured through the years, so did the things I learned to love and admire about her.

Judy was a woman of great loyalty – of great courage. What she has dealt with in recent years would have destroyed a lesser person – but she kept not only her steadfastness, but even her optimism – and always her sense of humor.

Judy was determined to live life to the fullest - and she did, practically to the very end. Her great joy in life was at the core of her being. And she was a woman who showed strong commitments. She was committed to her family in ways, and with a strength and consistency, which only they can fully know. There have been times of incredible pressure and stress, and she has always been there. And her granddaughter Sarah was the light of her life!

Judy was committed to her friends and community, and no one need detail what she has done for them. And, surely, she was also committed to herself. Almost to the end, she enjoyed her dancing, her theatre work, her playing in an orchestra. And she has, in all this, reminded me that I do not truly believe in death. Many of you may share my feelings – that as long as I am around, my light-hearted friend Judy will be a part of me."

In 1994, I lost my dear friend Helen. She had been failing for several years, and I had helped her to select a nursing home and plan for her final days. Though she had children, her relationship with them was somewhat strained, and I was in large part her caretaker. Helen had been such a good friend to me throughout the years and had done so much for me that it was a privilege to be able to help make her last months more comfortable. It made me particularly aware of my own good fortune, with supportive children and a large, close extended family. Helen had asked me to conduct her funeral – she was vaguely Protestant but, like Judy, she did not want a religious service. Again, I am inserting here the text of what I said.

"Good morning.

I'm Sarai Zitter – Helen's friend for over 37 years. This is what Helen wanted – not a religious service, but a gathering of family and friends to remember her, not in sorrow and mourning, but in celebration of a life lived to the fullest.

Also in keeping with her wishes, this is not a eulogy; we do not have to speak for a life which so richly speaks for itself. Rather, I am going to tell you a little of what our friendship has meant to me, and then I shall invite each of you to share your own recollections, stories and comments. Putting it all together will, I suspect, give us a well-rounded picture of the woman we are here to honor.

Helen certainly was outspoken. She could go right to the heart of a subject. The very first day I met her – in January 1957, collecting for the United Way, right after we both had moved into Cedar Grove – her daughter came down to say hello – asking if I had any children, because she baby-sat and loved children. Helen's remark – to this woman she had barely met – was, "It's true – Lexie does love children. She also loves money!" I don't know how fifteen-year-old Lexie felt about that, but my reaction was, "This is a woman I'll have to get to know!"

Helen was always there when I needed her. When I went to have my second child, it was Helen with whom I left my first. And when number three was arriving, it was Helen I called at 6 A.M. to stay with the other two. And thirty years later, when my mother was living with me before she died, it was Helen who had dinner with her, spent the night, visited in the afternoon – so that I could get out for a bit. Mother would never countenance a sitter- but Helen was a friend!

Helen was generous with her time and energy. Whether personally or professionally, she shared her wisdom and skills so that we all benefitted. When I started a co-op nursery school, Helen was our unpaid professional advisor. And, as my daughter reminded me yesterday, when she came to have coffee with me, she usually ended up folding laundry with me as well. An during these and later coffee-klatches, I came to know how deeply this very private woman cared for her children, and later, for her beloved grandchildren.

Helen had a car and hated to drive; I had none, but would drive anything with wheels. What a grand combination. Together we roamed the state, usually on mundane errands but sometimes for pure fun. We shared a love of flowers and long ago had formed the habit of going to the state Garden Show together. A few years back I started taking a wheelchair, and for the last few times we went she could not have managed without it. Our planned trip this year was cancelled by one of her many recent hospitalizations.

Helen was a fighter. If she believed something was right, she spoke up for it, not only in private conversations but in public forums as well. Many of you here can attest to her involvement with the community and her service to others during her later years. But she was always that way. And she was also a fighter in relation to her health – battling and defeating her cancer, and giving her thanks for her success by her active volunteer work in the St. Barnabas oncology service. However, I won't go any further into her varied volunteer work of recent years;

others here will, I know, do that.

To misquote Shakespeare, she was my friend – faithful and true to me. And to my children she was family, always sharing in our extended family activities. Without her, my life would have been barer; with her, it was enriched."

Then I invited those present to share their own recollections of Helen, starting with her children. I identified the charity to which she would have appreciated donations and invited them to a light lunch at my home nearby. I ended with this:

"I'd like to close with a little poem – I don't know who wrote it – that somehow feels appropriate.

> Do not stand at my grave and weep.
> I am not there; I do not sleep.
> I am a thousand winds that blow;
> I am the diamond glints on snow.
> I am the sunlight on ripened grain;
> I am the gentle autumn's rain.
> When you awaken in the morning's hush,
> I am the swift uplifting rush
> Of quiet birds in circled flight.
> I am the soft star that shines at night.
> Do not stand at my grave and cry.
> I am not there; I did not die."

Just a year later, I conducted the funeral for my lifelong friend, Judy Dvorkin. I must tell you about the Dvorkins, for Judy was as much my cousin as my friend. My mother and Judy's were college friends, and my father and Judy's were chums from high school days. My parents introduced her parents, and they were always Aunt Etta and Uncle Meyer to us. As their son Spencer was Barry's age and Judy just a year younger than I, we saw a lot of them. I recall a story of

175

when Judy was around four; her family was testing her on how well she understood the order of family relationships. "Why is Aunt Esther your aunt?" they asked. "Because she is Daddy's sister," came the reply. And why is Uncle Milton your uncle?" "Because he's Mommy's brother." Then came the trick question: "Why is Aunt Rose your aunt?" (Aunt Rose was my mother.) Quick as a wink came the reply, "She's our aunt because we love her!"

As the years passed, Spencer faded from my life, but Judy and I always remained close. She was a professional musician, writing songs, musical plays and many other works. Judy never married, but took pleasure in trying out her children's musicals on my children. They loved having her visit; she brought a spark of a magical world into our suburban home, and her piano playing showed them something of what it was possible to achieve. In addition to the fascinating stories she had to tell of the musical and theatre world, she really listened to the children and showed genuine interest in all their activities.

Judy also died of cancer, but had been careful not to let me know she was failing. She was afraid I would insist on bringing her out to my house and taking care of her (how right she was!) and – typically – didn't want to inconvenience me. She left me all her jewelry and, more importantly, she left my whole family with warm and loving memories.

With the help of some of her musician friends, we arranged a funeral where her music was played softly all during the proceedings. Again, following her wishes, I officiated. You will note that I used many of the same concepts here as in my previous eulogy. Here is what I said:

"Good evening. I'm Sarai Zitter – Judy's friend for over

sixty-seven years. This is what Judy would have wanted – not a religious service, but a gathering of family and friends to remember her not in sorrow and mourning, but in celebration of a life lived to the fullest.

Also in keeping with what she would have wished, this is not a eulogy. We do not have to speak for a life which so richly speaks for itself. Rather, I am going to tell you a little of what our friendship has meant to me, and then I shall invite each of you to share some of your own recollections, stories and comments. Putting it all together will, I suspect, give us a well-rounded picture of the woman we are here to remember.

Outside of her immediate family and my own brother, I have known Judy longer than did anyone else. Our mothers were college friends; our fathers, friends since high school. My parents introduced her parents. The Dvorkins were part of my extended family, growing up – and Judy has been family for my own children. She hated crowds – would have refused to attend a gathering such as this one – but when we had just our family she loved to join us, often schlepping to and from Jersey by bus. She brought her enthusiasm, her keen interest in all our activities, her tales and stories of life in the world of theatre – and always, she brought her music. She previewed for my children many of the songs and lyrics she wrote for children's productions; she shared much of the cultural richness, as well as funny stories, of the world in which she lived. With generosity of spirit she shared in our lives and made each of us feel 'special.'

It is close to fifty years ago that Judy taught me to play the guitar – a skill which I took pleasure in passing on to my own children – and went with me to purchase my instrument. You will believe the time frame when I tell you that I paid most of my summer's earnings – seventy dollars – for that Martin, which is currently appraised at $1,600. As you can see, she didn't steer me wrong.

You all know how hard a worker Judy was. When she was involved in a project, she focused on it seven days a week. Yet she was available to mentor younger colleagues, and for more than one served as a role model.

Judy was a very private person. Many of you have told me how interested she was in you, yet how little she shared with you of her personal life. And this was true even with her nearest and dearest. She was fiercely independent, too – dare I say stubborn? – and these are the traits which led to *nobody* being aware of her illness until a brief few days before her death. Her two main goals, at the end, were to maintain control over her own life and not to give anybody unneeded trouble!

With great difficulty I am going to resist the temptation to expound on other of Judy's traits and talents – and that restraint is only because I know that many of you here will want to do that. Also, no expression of Judy's life would be complete without including her music, and some of her friends have seen to it that music is a part of this memorial.

To misquote Shakespeare, she was my friend – faithful and true to me. Without her, my life would have been barer; with her, it was enriched.

And now, I'd like to ask each of you to share whatever comments and recollections to which you feel inspired. And we'll start with Judy's brother, Spencer."

After many people had spoken, I concluded with:
"Thank you all. You should know that the incidental music you heard earlier was provided by Dick Lieb, and the later

songs by Wayne Blood. In each case, Judy was either the composer or the lyricist.

Just a final announcement: if any of you wish to make a memorial contribution, it may be sent either to Life Line for the Old in Israel or to The United Negro College Fund, Judy's two favorite charities. The addresses are available on your way out.

I'd like to close with a poem which somehow feels appropriate to Judy's strength of will, her independence – and yes, her stubbornness – Invictus.

> Out of the night which covers me,
> Black as the pit from pole to pole,
> I thank whatever gods there be
> For my unconquerable soul.
>
> In the fell clutch of circumstance,
> I have not winced nor cried aloud.
> Under the bludgeoning of chance
> My head is bloody, but unbowed.
>
> Beyond this place of wrath and tears
> Looms but the horror of the shade.
> And yet, the menace of the years
> Finds, and shall find me, unafraid.
>
> It matters not how strait the gate,
> How charged with punishment the scroll.
> I am the Master of my fate.
> I am the Captain of my soul.
>
> Thank you all for coming."

You can well believe that I was more than happy to switch

from funerals to a wedding. But first, a bit of background. As I have mentioned, Sam and I had family on the west coast. His next older brother, Itch, had two children, Richard and Arlene, living in California. While a family misunderstanding had, to Sam's great sorrow, caused a rift with Richard (since mended), we were always close to Arlene and her daughters. When the older one, Heather, was looking at colleges we took her around to see several in the East, and her selection of Tufts started four years of her spending most of the holidays with us. We became very close, and she was able to observe the quality of our marriage, very different from that of her own parents.

Fast forward to 2009. Heather had met her future husband on the east coast, and they had maintained their relationship across three thousand miles. Perhaps because it was a religiously mixed marriage, they opted to ask what they termed their 'role models' to officiate at their wedding. This meant Jesse's uncle and me. I cannot imagine a more meaningful compliment, and that occasion remains one of the high spots of my life. I enjoyed researching the history of the ketubah for them, and gloried in my awareness that it was not so much me as an individual, but Sam's and my marriage, which Heather so wished to emulate.

I am inserting here the welcome which I gave on that occasion, as well as the "Words of Wisdom" which each of us was invited to supply.

WELCOME

"What a privilege - what an honor – to welcome you all on this auspicious occasion! Heather and Jesse are getting married! I'm sure you all felt as thrilled as I did when you were invited to share in this celebration. But our bride and groom are also honored by your presence. They exchange their vows tonight surrounded by your love and sustained by your support. The loving home which they establish will surely be enriched by your participation here today.

In the name of Heather and Jesse and of their families, I bid you welcome."

And then, later in the service:

Words of Wisdom
"What a treat – to actually be asked for advice! I'll try to make the most of it. There are probably as many kinds of marriages as there are couples involved in them. And yet, thinking about what to say tonight, I found a few basic ideas coming to the fore – things which probably are common to most successful relationships.

We can pass quickly over love. Love is a given here. It is the basis for this marriage and serves as the grease on the wheels of daily interactions. If it were not palpably a part of Heather and Jesse's relationship, we would not be here this evening. But tonight we take love to a new level – commitment. There is an important difference between courtship and marriage. In the former, one may see a problem and wonder if you will be able to solve it. In the latter, the question is how you will solve it; commitment means that you know you will, you must, find a way.

Respect – this is easy when we see eye to eye, but perhaps more demanding where our experiences, our preferences or tastes lead us in different directions. No two people will agree on everything – and that's fortunate, or we would miss out on the broader outlook, the wider horizon which differing viewpoints can provide. But to disagree, one need not be disagreeable. And respectful, courteous listening helps each of you to feel comfortable with your eventual decisions.

Did I say courteous? Remember the old line, "Love is never having to say you're sorry?" Well, don't believe it for a minute! It's amazing how many people fail to treat their nearest and dearest with the simple good manners which they would extend to a stranger. Of course, those of us who have seen Jesse and Heather together are completely at ease in this area.

Every treatise one reads makes mention of communication. This is a two-way street, involving both a sender and a receiver. It doesn't matter how eloquently a message is phrased; if it is not able to be heard, communication has not taken place. It goes without saying that we are honest with each other. A loving relationship makes it possible to admit mistakes and disappointments with the expectation of support rather than criticism. In this, our home becomes a true haven from the many stresses of the world. There is a magical mathematics to this – while a burden shared is thereby diminished, a triumph shared becomes bigger and brighter. And of course, the whole – the relationship – is greater than the sum of its parts.

There is no need to emphasize togetherness. It is basically the reason we get married. But what does it mean? There is a romantic notion that we become merged, as two halves of a whole. I would warn you against that. It would diminish you both. You are two separate people. It is your uniqueness which attracted you to one another; do not lose your own selves in the joy of your togetherness. Caring for one another must not diminish the importance of caring also for yourselves.

Let me borrow the words of the poet Gibran:
"Together you shall be forevermore.
You shall be together when the white wings of death scatter your days.

Aye, you shall be together even in the silent memory of God.
But let there be spaces in your togetherness,
And let the winds of the heavens dance between you.

Love one another, but make not a bond of love:
Let it rather be a moving sea between the shores of your souls.
Sing and dance together and be joyous, but let each one of you be alone,
Even as the strings of a lute are alone though they quiver with the same music.

And stand together yet not too near together,
For the pillars of the temple stand apart,
And the oak tree and the cypress grow not in each other's shadow."

As I look for inspiration to my own fifty years of happy marriage, I realize I've almost left out a very important element – fun! There's not much point in anything if you can't find ways to enjoy it. You will work together, struggle together, build a family and a life together - but leave room to play together, too. Laughter has been found to be good for your health – well, it's good for your marriage, too. A little humor can lighten many a dark moment, and laughter can frequently defuse tense ones.

And speaking of tense moments - they'll come to you, as they do to all of us – but you have here a template for facing them. With loving commitment, with mutual respect, with open communication and trust, with the sure knowledge that the 'us' is greater than the 'you' and the 'me', you will find that you emerge stronger and wiser, with your love and your commitment intact. And as you live this experience, you may find that caring for yourself and caring for one another, giving and receiving, feel increasingly similar, merely two steps in your joyous dance.

Your union enlarges you, encourages growth in each of you. And if you think your beloved is terrific now, I have good news for you. As you grow and your relationship matures, I can assure you that this perception will only be enhanced by the passing years.

Thank you both, Heather and Jesse, for giving me the privilege of sharing this occasion with you."

CHAPTER XXVI: DOGS AND MORE DOGS - AND CATS, TOO

In the course of a lifetime, many things take place which the family finds amusing or interesting. Fortunately, Sam and I were both paper-savers, so my memory can be jogged in relation to some of them.

I have mentioned our fondness for dogs. Of course, when we went camping, the dog always came along. But there were occasional trips which were not pet-friendly. My cousins, Judi and Lee, were happy to provide care for Shadow on one such occasion. We met in New York City to switch him from our car to theirs, and then proceeded on our way. Judi and Lee had small children, and warned them about keeping Shadow in the house – but naturally, one of them held the door open as he was talking to his parents outside, and Shadow was off at a run. He was wearing a license, of course, but the phone number to be called was ours – and nobody was at home there. Judi and Lee each headed off in a different direction, calling for Shadow. Finally Lee spotted him at the other end of a large playing field; there was no way he could get to him without the dog taking off. But Lee remembered my bragging how well-trained Shadow was; he called out firmly, "Shadow, sit!" – and Shadow obediently plopped down on his rear and waited for Lee to slip a leash on him.

It was Robin who had trained him. When we had our first dog, Frisky and I had gone together to training classes at the adult school. It was highly successful, and we wanted Shadow to have a similar opportunity. Though we all loved animals, Robin was particularly devoted to them, and Sam and I felt it would be good for her to be involved in this training. As the youngest, she sometimes felt deprived of some privilege accorded to the older ones, and this would be something which she had which the others did not. Also, as it is the trainer rather than the dog who is actually being trained, we felt this structure might also be of benefit to her. So when we heard the story of how Lee recaptured Shadow, we made sure the credit went to Robin.

Lee and Judi had a dog, Jackson, who actually belonged to the Foundation for the Blind. They had fostered him as a puppy, and when he was ready to be given to a blind person, the foundation decided to keep him for stud – so Lee and Judi were able to continue fostering him for the next nine years. As Judi put it, every few months he would spend a weekend at the Foundation, and come home brushed and combed and with a smile on his face. But when he was nine, he was considered too old for stud, and Lee and Judi were able actually to adopt him.

But now came a new problem; until then, when they went on vacation, Jackson went to his home kennel. But now the dog was theirs; his 'home kennel' was their house. The Foundation also previously had paid for his medical care, but this was not an issue. Sam and I overheard them discussing this at a family gathering, and volunteered to take Jackson for the three weeks they were to be away. So they sent him to Camp Zitter, and when he went home we sent along a camp report, here reproduced in its entirety.

Camp Zitter
16 Reservoir Place
Cedar Grove, NJ 07009

re: Paseltiner, Jackson
This report may be incomplete, due to short notice.

Jackson has been a model camper. His socialization skills are superior; he is consistently outgoing and friendly, even affectionate, yet is able to entertain himself quietly when appropriate. He shows a strong literary bent, perhaps not surprising when one considers his lineage; it is demonstrated by the frequency with which he likes to curl up by the bookcase.

Although personally non-aggressive, he can be aroused by aggressive overtures on the part of passing strangers - residents of other camps, that is - but is readily restrained from putting his angry feelings into action. What this inhibition costs him in terms of emotional distress can be, of course, only a matter of conjecture.

Jackson has excellent personal habits. His meals are consumed with dispatch, and there have been no reports of his involvement in food fights. Though Jackson clearly enjoys extra treats, he does not whine or beg for them; he shows his appreciation, however, when a treat is proffered. Toileting behavior is also well-disciplined and appropriate.

Visitors as well as staff find Jackson to be a welcome addition to our camp family. All in all, he has proven to be a model camper.

Should facilities be available at our new location, we would certainly look favorably on an application for a campership in 1996.

Camp CO-Director
Camp CO-Director
Date: August 19, 1995

Sarai G. Zitter

We enjoyed Jackson, and he earned his keep; Judi had
alerted me, and I gave him a package to carry in when I had
been shopping, to his obvious pleasure and pride. He also
brought in our newspaper each morning. Sometimes, he
even brought us our neighbor's newspaper as well. All in
all, we were delighted to have him return the next summer.
As it happened, we had moved to Monroe Township during
that winter, but Jackson adapted readily to his new quarters.
George Lewin, our new neighbor, took a particular liking to
Jackson and when we were out for any reason, George was
happy to feed and walk him. Our next camp report appears
below.

Camp Zitter
5 Stiring Circle
Jamesburg, NJ 08831

re: Paseltiner, Jackson

It was a pleasure to welcome Jackson back to camp. He has
been a model camper in the past, and we expected no less
of him this year.

Despite our change of location, Jackson settled in readily
in his new quarters. Though his personal habits are, as
always, excellent, he does demonstrate a certain
disinclination to spend the entire night in his own bed,
frequently preferring the floor near one or another
counselor. On the other hand, he will use his bed readily
for naps, especially when an adult is nearby. One might
comment that he gives a whole new meaning to the phrase
"dogging one's footsteps".

Due to his advanced age Jackson was placed in our senior
unit this year. Athletic activities were limited, in keeping
with his arthritic tendencies, but he still enjoyed several

188

daily constitutionals, always supervised by a counselor.
He became quite well known in the surrounding community,
was greeted by name by an increasing number of friends
along the way, and made numerous attempts to enter homes
uninvited. However, he accepted restraint with equanimity.
It should be noted that he had younger friends as well,
comprising the many visiting grandchildren at surrounding
campsites.

Jackson made a particular friend of the counselor next
door. In fact, he gave him a farewell gift, to show his
appreciation for the many times the latter accompanied him
on evening strolls when his primary caretakers were
unavailable.

Perhaps because of his advancing years, Jackson did quite a
good bit of resting during the day. However, he was always
eager for planned exercise, and performed his chores with
dispatch. (One should be aware that we get not one, but
two newspapers daily.) Unfortunately, he does not appear to
appreciate their literary content.

The entire camping community will miss Jackson. The hope
has been expressed in several quarters that he will plan to
return to camp next year.

Camp Co-Director
Camp Co-Director

Alas, he did not return. Jackson died that year of old age,
and was mourned by far more than just his immediate family.

Another pet story – in both senses of the word – is about
Shadow's stint as a baby-sitter. We had adopted a tiger-striped
kitten, after the classic 'she followed me home' story. In this
case, it was true; she showed up on our doorstep one summer
day, and we took her in. She and Shadow became fast friends.

In fact, when I took Shadow for a walk, Tigerlily (so named for the orange splash on her forehead) would often accompany us part way before disappearing into the bushes on business of her own. It was startling to strangers to see this huge collie bossed around by our little cat. When Tigerlily became pregnant, she made a nest in the bottom of Robin's closet (I kept asking Robin why her bathrobe always ended up on the floor, little realizing that it was Tiger's doing). When she was ready to give birth, she evidently wanted family support, for she came mewing to us, indicating that she wanted us to follow her; she gave birth in the closet, on the bathrobe, with Sam taking movie pictures of the entire event. Shadow was immediately pressed into service as sitter.

Needless to say, we had provided a box for the kittens. Whenever Tiger left the box, whether to eat, use the litter box, or go outside, Shadow would take over. He plopped his big, black, furry paw into the box; the kittens would scramble over it, nip, play, whatever, but Shadow remained faithfully at his post until Tiger returned. Would that all baby-sitters were so responsible.

We had, of course, renewed our contract with Agnes several times, so that she had been with us for four years when she got married. When we were giving away the kittens, Agnes wanted the orange male, so we kept it for her. Though I would have called him Marmalade, Agnes opted for Toodles, so Toodles he became. It turned out that their first apartment did not permit pets, so he remained with us. Now when I walked Shadow, I had a parade! Shadow walked behind me at heel; Tigerlily slinked sinuously behind him, while Toodles bounced along in her wake. When we reached the corner, the two cats would disappear into the bushes, but however long or short our walk, on our way home they would come join us for the last lap of the journey. I wish we had movies of *that*. When we had gotten Shadow, Agnes and her fiancé, Wayne, had gotten one of his litter-brothers. Wayne kept him until their marriage and then, because of the no-pet apartment rule, gave him to his brother. Skippy was suddenly orphaned when Wayne's brother was killed in an auto accident. Shadow was at that time ill with a kidney condition; it was obvious that he would not live much longer. I could not even imagine what his death would do to Robin, and partly for that reason, partly because we were concerned for the dog, we brought Skippy into our home. For a few months we had the two dogs; they looked startlingly alike, though Shadow looked particularly frail next to his husky, healthy brother. As we had anticipated, Shadow did not survive much longer, and though the whole family was desolate, I do believe that having Skippy really helped all of us, especially Robin.

Some years later, when Robin was at Bates College, she took Skippy with her, arranging for living quarters other than in a dorm. One afternoon I was sitting in the kitchen with a cup of coffee when the door opened, and in walked Robin. I took one look at her face and said, "Oh, Robin, it's Skippy!" Skippy had died; Robin had lugged the forty pound animal downstairs, taken him to the vet for cremation, and then got in her car and drove straight home! Just seeing her face, somehow I knew!

Sarai G. Zitter

CHAPTER XXVII: THE KIDS ARE ON THEIR OWN

Robin chose to switch from Bates to the New York School of Horticulture, so she was back at home again. Sherry had remained in the Boston area, working there until she decided on graduate school plans. Mark decided he wanted to try the west coast for a while, and began looking for a job in California. Sam was the family specialist in resume writing – he had helped many friends and family members with this throughout the years – and Mark sent us a copy of his resume for suggestions, with the following cover letter:

Box 1174 Wesleyan Station
Middletown, Conn, 16457
February 25, 1980

Mr, and Mrs. Samuel Zitter
16 Reservoir Place
Cedar Grove, N.J. 07009

Dear Mr. and Mrs. Zitter:

I am a senior at Wesleyan and would like to join your staff at the position of number one son. I learned of the opening through your advertisement in the New York Times, and also by word of mouth.

I have heard of your reputation as nifty parents, and feel that I could easily fit into your organization in a manner beneficial to us all. As *for* my qualifications, I come from a very good background.

I have enclosed a copy of my resume, as well as three letters of recommendation. I hope that you feel that my credentials are worthy of such a position as the one you are offering.

I hope that we can set up an interview at a mutually convenient time. I will be in New Jersey during the latter half of March, and will be in touch with you at that time. I look forward to meeting with you.

Very truly yours,
Mark R. Zitter

I responded as follows:

Hospitality Office
16 Reservoir Place
Cedar Grove, NJ 07009
February 26, 1980

Mr. Mark R. Zitter
Box 1174
Wesleyan Station
Middletown, Conn. 16457

Dear Mr. Zitter:

Your letter of Feb. 25th arrived today, and received considerable positive attention. It is not our policy to offer employment without extensive individual assessment and interviewing of the applicant; however, your resume is indeed impressive, and I do have rather a favorable impression from our earlier, though informal, contacts. However, I must call to your attention that you neglected to enclose the letters of recommendation which you mentioned; was this an oversight, or were you unable to find anyone to say a good word for you?

In any event, due as much to the excellent family reputation to which you are heir, as to the detailed and well-prepared resume which you enclose, we have decided to select you for the opening described – but on a trial basis only, of course.

193

Sarai G. Zitter

If your performance proves as satisfactory as we anticipate, however, we will be prepared to offer you a contract for a permanent position. Number One Son is surely an honor worth aspiring to! And a preposition is something you must never end a sentence with!

We will discuss responsibilities and compensation during our March interview.

It has been our practice to offer home hospitality to employees – and spouse, if any – when first you come to New Jersey. This gives you the opportunity to obtain more permanent quarters, and gives us the chance to get to know you better. Please let me know the size of your present family, so I may make appropriate arrangements.

Compensation is substantial for this position, ranging from tuition for college courses and medical insurance, to emotional support, meals on and off the road, and family guidance and counseling. Responsibilities, of course, are commensurate with the above, including such far-flung activities as painting ceilings, reaching material on high shelves, and Basic Household Chores; familiarity with lawn mower, snow shovel, and creative dishwashing techniques is also considered an asset. Courses in the above – in-depth courses, in fact, with practicum included – are available with (or without) request. Additional responsibilities may be added without notice.

We look forward to a mutually satisfactory relationship, and hope that it will last for many years. Incidentally, you will be interested to know that after 25 years of uninterrupted service, our employees may consider that any and all options have been picked up, and they need no longer fear termination of contract.

Sincerely yours,
Sarai G. Zitter
SGZ/sgz for the firm

Though the children came and went during the ensuing years, we never again had our basic family of five living together at home. It was always a joy to have them visit, but we never suffered from the famous "empty nest" syndrome. Life was always busy. In addition to our work and organizational activities, Sam and I enjoyed travel, and were fortunate in being able to visit many of the places we wanted to see. We stayed with Peggy and Phil in Japan. We visited (for Sam, revisited) the area in China where he had spent the wartime years; we went to Spain, traveling on Sam's ability to speak Spanish (we took Robin with us on that one); we had a wonderful three week driving and bed-and-breakfast trip through England and Scotland, and we were joined by Molly and Alex on a trip through Scandinavia. With Irma and Arnold, we went to Alaska, with Judi and Lee to Ireland, and to celebrate our joint retirement we traveled to Costa Rica.

I should mention that Sam had not planned on going to Japan. Our friend Phil had several one-year stints there as an exchange professor, and the second time they went I decided to visit. In the past, I had always been glad to go anywhere Sam chose, so when he said Japan was not a place he was interested in visiting, he apparently thought that would end the matter. "All right," I said. "I can go by myself." It didn't take long for Sam to decide to join me – and we both had a wonderful time. At one point we stayed in a Buddhist Temple, one of those which Phil was researching for a book he later wrote. The young monk who served as our guide knew a little English; when he showed us to our adjoining rooms, I looked at the huge quilt-covered futon and said, "That's big enough for the four of us!" The monk was shocked beyond measure. "No, no," he protested. "Two here, two there; no four together." We were so amused that we set the camera for a self-photo and then arranged ourselves on one of the futons, under the cover, in mixed-up order so that we were next to one another's spouses. We called it "Four On A Futon", and had poster-sized copies made for their six children and our three. A copy of that picture appears in Phil's later-published book.

It was shortly after that time that we brought my mother out to live with us. She and Aunt Anna had been sharing an apartment at Kittay House in the Bronx. Kittay was a senior apartment house, a prototype of the Independent Living facility which has become so popular today. They had moved there soon after Dad's death, and found it to be a thoroughly satisfactory arrangement. But Mother began showing signs of senility, and I feared that she would bring Aunt Anna down with her as this progressed. Mother had earlier resisted our invitation to live with us, but now she seemed ready. It was sad to see this independent, competent woman become unsure of herself and emotionally dependent. When Mother was 82 she resigned as treasurer of the Hunter College Scholarship and Welfare Association, where she had been managing a two million dollar investment portfolio. At 85, she was still doing taxes for her neighbors at Kittay House. But by the time she was 87 I had to take over her checkbook; she was no longer capable of managing it herself.

We were fortunate that this happened after the children were grown and on their own. We never suffered from the "sandwich generation" effect that burden so many families; we were able to look after Mother as we felt was needed, without being torn by conflicting demands. Yes, it was hard seeing her deteriorate before our eyes, but she had been such an incredibly competent, supportive, giving person that Sam and I both felt it was a privilege to care for her. Also, we had both retired from our principal jobs by then, so our time was more flexible.

Sam had always wanted to retire early, to have time for writing, and that is what he did. All through the years we had saved his bonuses, planning for the leaner years before he would begin to collect Social Security. He had taken some courses in writing at nearby colleges, and I suggested that, as he had never gotten a college degree, he might want to see how many of his old credits he could recapture, possibly focusing his courses toward a BA. He contacted both City College and NYU, finding that he had over two years worth of credits still available. With the credit given for life experience, obtaining a college degree seemed quite realistic. With his typical determination, he forged ahead, majoring in English and building his curriculum around his passion for writing. One college requirement is physical education. How was he to meet that? Well, Sam had been – in fact, still was – an avid and skilled tennis player. The college accepted affidavits to that effect to meet his phys ed requirement.

CHAPTER XXVIII: JUST US TWO

To return to Greenbriar days: when we first moved there, Sam noted that it had no Chapter of the Jewish Federation. Having been active in the past as a fundraiser both for Federation and for United Way, he saw this as a gap which needed closing. With a couple of others, particularly George Lewin and Harold Lazar, he started a Chapter and served as its first president. I was involved in a number of other organizations, but after Sam's death in 2003 I joined the board of Greenbriar's Federation, feeling the need to keep involved in what had been such an important part of his life. At one point, Federation had wanted to honor us both at an annual meeting; I demurred at being included, feeling that it was Sam alone who had been so active. They accepted this and he was awarded a plaque, as was Harold, who had co-founded the Chapter with him. Later, after Sam and I purchased a charitable annuity for Federation, I allowed them to include me in the publicity and award, hoping that it would encourage others to do likewise. But after I had been on the board for a few years, I was again asked to accept an award, in honor of my lifelong volunteerism. This was, for me, a truly rewarding experience, as I went back through my papers and pulled out recollections of activities which I had almost forgotten. I wished that Sam could have been there to share in the occasion - I wished he could have been there to introduce me! - but I was nonetheless delighted to have Sherry assume that role. I shall insert here both her words of introduction, and my response. First, however, let me offer a copy of my volunteer history which appeared on the program:

Sarai Zitter – July 2007

What a fortunate life I have led. During World War II I spent summers farming for the Women's Land Army on a save-the-crops mission. When our janitor was called into the Navy, I took over, shoveling coal daily at 5 AM .

My husband and I spent our courtship on a sound-truck for Adlai Stevenson, Sam giving speeches and I, with my guitar, singing political songs. Alas, our candidate lost – but we won, the prize being our fifty years of happy marriage.

When my three children were small, I organized and ran a cooperative nursery school. I served as and helped to train Girl Scout leaders. As a board member of the Mental Health Resource Center, I worked on their overnight hotline for twenty years.

I organized a Fair Housing Committee which effectively integrated my town of Cedar Grove. Dare I admit that I was arrested and handcuffed by the Washington police while demonstrating against apartheid – a recollection which I treasure!

I've been an activist for women's rights throughout my life, with reproductive rights taking center stage. I was board president of NJ Right To Choose, frequently representing that organization in high school and college presentations. I also served as pregnancy options counselor for Planned Parenthood in Trenton. Currently I am giving a workshop series on Parenting Adult Children, under the auspices of Hadassah.

I've served or now serve on the boards of my temple, Etz Chaim, the Monroe Township League of Women Voters, and presently am VP of Social Action in the Clearbrook section of the National Council of Jewish Women. As a Board member for the Greenbriar Division of Federation (a group of which my husband was a prime organizer)I co-wrote the By-Laws and serve as Parliamentarian.

I graduated from Wellesley College, and received masters degrees from the University of Michigan and Simmons School of Social Work. I bore three children, acquired a wonderful daughter-in-law, and am blessed with three grandchildren.

It's been a busy, satisfying life. But hey! – I'm only eighty-one. Who knows what the future may hold?

This is Sherry's introduction of me:

"Hello, I'm Sarai's elder daughter, Sherry.

I recently sent a card to my mother because it epitomized her: It was the Chinese proverb "The one who says it cannot be done should not interrupt the one doing it."

When we were growing up, one of my mother's favorite expressions was: "The difficult we can do immediately; the impossible takes a little longer." This is how she has lived her life and helped us to live ours. When she sets her mind to something, I believe there is nothing Mother cannot do, and with great integrity - - whether it be integrating the town of Cedar Grove in the 1960's, escaping from the Welsh Botanical gardens with me a few years ago by climbing over a high fence, or improving social justice and the human condition in all of the numerous ways she has served during her rich lifetime -- so far!

Born to a suffragist mother with a strong tradition of lifetime volunteerism, and a pediatrician father who saw many families without charge during the depression, Mother continued their rich tradition of service. From creating a cooperative nursery school to teaching wilderness and self-sufficiency skills to scores of Girl Scouts, Mother saw what was needed for her own children and others, and has responded generously. On more than one occasion while we were growing up, she took in friends of teenagers who were struggling and needed a "home away from home" for a while, nurturing them lovingly until they got back on track.

Mother has a gift for seeing the deep interconnections among the character development of youth, human rights, social and environmental justice and community service at the local, state, national and global levels. These visions have inspired all of her children in the lives we now lead: my sister in her work protecting the environment, my brother and sister-in-law in Jewish affairs and community service, and my work towards global peace, which many see as an impossible dream, but my mother's vision of doing the impossible has made an incurable optimist out of me! As Gandhi exhorted, we are all "being the change we wish to see in the world," as Mother's life example has encouraged us to do.

As children, we were taught mutual respect and sharing as early life lessons. At age 5, we each were started on a weekly allowance of 15 cents: 5 for savings, 5 for spending and 5 for charity, or tsedakah. Watching those charitable nickels mount up and being given choices as to which cause to donate are among my earliest memories of feeling good about myself. In fact, my mother recalls that when I returned home from my first babysitting job at age 11 with $2, my first question to her was: "Do you think 10% is enough to give to charity?"

When my brother lost a toy boat carrying a soldier into a large sewer pipe at the end of our backyard stream and went upset to my mother, wanting to see if it would reappear a few miles down the road, she loaded us up immediately in the car and waited patiently with us at the next opening --and it reappeared! When my 6 year old sister was drawing a horse and asked my mother to draw the head for her, my mother, with no talent for art, said "I don't think 1 can;" and my well-trained

201

sister said: "You can try." So try she did, and Robin said "I can do better than that" and did so! Mother believed fully in each of us, so a deep belief in ourselves came naturally, along with a sense of joyful responsibility toward others and toward our Earth. Mother raised "can-do" children -- each of us as well as her daughter-in-law is an entrepreneur, involved variously in creating ecologically sustainable plant communities to improving health, mental health and end-of-life care -- and each follow her rich lifelong example of donating substantial time and money to the causes in which we most believe -- as her grandchildren are being taught to do as well.

For Mother, giving of herself to those who need her, whether family or stranger, is of a piece. She truly lives the injunction from Deuteronomy to welcome "the stranger within thy gates" and has a way of including all of humanity and nature in her respect and affection that continues to teach all of us so much. She has a large circle of devoted admirers from both younger generations of our family who feel her as an extra mother or grandmother because of her strong devotion to them throughout the years.

I'll end with a brief poem by Edwin Markham that characterizes Mother better than any other, entitled "Outwitted:"

You drew a circle that shut me out
Heretic, rebel, a thing to flout.
But love and I had the wit to win:
We drew a circle that took you in.

"Mother, we are all so proud and delighted to be here with you today!"

And my acceptance:

"As I looked back through my life history in preparation
for this honor, I realized two great truths, which I would like
to share with you. The first is that, no matter how active, how
generous, how service-directed we may try to be, we always
get back more than we give. All these activities which I
thought I was doing for the sake of others are the very things
which have most enhanced and enriched my own life, and
led me down paths to the greatest satisfactions and the most
important relationships.

The second is that none of us stands alone. I was struck by
the invisible thread which connects each of us to the past and to
the future. I thought of my immigrant grandmother's pishkes
-. for those of us old enough to remember what that means -
lined up in her kitchen, into which would go two cents for the
Hebrew School, three cents for the Jewish National Fund. I
think of my mother, who marched for women's suffrage, and
then helped to develop the League of Women Voters - and the
Bronx Girl Scouts-- and who helped create the Hunter College
Scholarship and Welfare Fund, knowing that had there been
a fee, she could not have attended college. And I look with
pride and affection at my children - at the daughter who works
for the welfare of animals, and serves on her town's Wetlands
Commission, protecting the environment and beautifying
her little corner of our endangered earth; and at the son who
still serves the college from which he graduated 25 years
ago, and who, with his wife, works to support and enhance
their children's school and their family's synagogue, opening
their hearts and their checkbooks to those in need; and at the
daughter who works for the rights of those disenfranchised
by poverty, disability, or sexual orientation, and presents
programs working toward world peace; and I look at my three
grandchildren, already showing awareness of their own good
fortune, and of their obligations towards others. None of us

stands alone. And so it is in the name of all these that I thank you for this great honor."

My family and friends were there, of course, and we found a way to include my grandchildren in some of the activities. I might add that the large glass plaques which Federation gives out on such occasions represent a problem of storage, now that I am in smaller quarters. After all, between Sam and me, I now have three of them to house.

CHAPTER XXIX: LOSS

Before I write of Sam's demise, I want to mention some important prior losses. The first was Dad's mother, Bubby, who died when I was in Social Work school. She lived next door to us, and we were close. It was my first significant experience of loss. Bubby Shagan, Mother's foster mother, had died when I was about nine, and though she was important to us, she had lived at a distance and I saw her only occasionally. But Bubby Golomb, gentle and loving, was an integral part of my every-day life. I might mention an amusing side-item here: we all thought she was seventy-eight, but when her daughters went through her papers after her death, it turned out that she was actually seventy-nine. She was a few months older than her husband (who died when I was an infant) and had dropped a year when she arrived in America so that she would be a few months younger.

Bubby had written a holographic will, in Yiddish, much of which was pure poetry and which showed her loving spirit. She had little of value to leave, but mentioned her five necklaces. She spoke of her four daughters – the tzugebornene and the tzugevornene – ie, those who were born to her and those who had come to her. One necklace was for each, and the fifth was for me, her oldest granddaughter. My aunts let me choose first, and I selected her jets, which she had called her "mourning beads". I wear and treasure them to this day.

Bubby, who had taught me to crochet lace, also left me a gift which I did not know about until I was engaged to Sam. Long troubled by my lack of a 'hope chest', she had made me a linen tablecloth edged with crochet, and with large crocheted lace corners, with napkins to match. She had given it to my mother to keep, saying, "If I'm around when Sissy gets married, I'll give this to her. Otherwise, you give it to her from me." I still get choked up when I tell of it. And it gave me an idea! I am currently knitting an afghan for each of my grandchildren. I will leave them with the same instructions: if I'm here when they graduate from high school, I will give it to them; otherwise, one of my children will give it to them as a gift from me. Incidentally, when Bubby died she was in the midst of crocheting a set of lace antimacassars for my Aunt Shully. I was the only one in the family who had learned lace-making from Bubby, and I finished the set. Everyone was very much impressed, declaring that they could not see where Bubby's work left off and mine began. But I could tell; Bubby's work, at age 79, was still finer than mine.

My next major loss was of my father, who died at eighty-one. Although he was no longer robust, it was a sudden and unexpected death; he had fallen down a staircase while at a meeting, and died instantly. It was the day after Yom Kippur, so almost his entire family had been together the previous evening to break the fast. The suddenness was a shock to us all, but Mother coped with this loss of her husband of fifty-three years with the dignity and grace which characterized her entire life.

When Mother died, my loss was far greater. This was for two reasons. First, she and I had always been very close. I identified with her, modeled myself on her, and considered it a compliment when people thought I was like her. Our values and beliefs were very similar, and she was always my staunch supporter and ally. Second, she had lived with me for the past year, and my life had been in large part built around her care. There was a large time gap to be filled again with the many activities which had temporarily been put on hold.

Another loss was that of my well-loved sister-in-law, Bobbie. We had met when she was not yet twenty, and I barely twenty-one. Though different in many ways, we shared a love of family and a youthful joie de vivre which matured into a lifelong friendship. I had entertained a vague notion of us as two old ladies, widowed and looking after one another. Her early death was truly a blow.

But to me, of course, none of these losses compared to that of Sam. He had a number of health problems during his last few years, including an abdominal aneurism and colorectal cancer. The chemotherapy and radiation for the latter were debilitating. Possibly as a result of the radiation, he developed an aberrant form of leukemia, and we had regular runs to New York for various experimental treatments. But the time came when he did not have the strength for the trip. We were fortunate in being able to have him remain at home. Much credit goes to my daughter-in-law for this privilege. Jess was visiting us the day Sam could not make the trip to New York, and the doctor there told me to take him to his local doctor. His oncologist in turn directed me to take him to the emergency room, where he would be worked up, tested, etc. Jess pictured for me what would happen: he was in such poor condition that they would admit him, and he almost certainly would never be well enough to be discharged. Oxygen might prolong his life by a few days, but he would die in the hospital, breathing through a tube. Was this what we wanted? The alternative was clearly our choice.

With the help of Hospice, Sam was kept reasonably comfortable and at ease. I was put in charge of his medication and used the morphine as needed to keep him pain-free. A hospital bed was moved into our room, next to my bed, so that we could continue to fall asleep holding hands. When we were younger, it was in each other's arms – but the stiffness

207

of advancing age and arthritis had shifted that pleasant pattern to hand-holding.

Despite discomfort and physical deterioration, Sam retained his personality to the end – his warmth, his sweetness of nature, and even his sense of humor. He was surprised that it took so long to die. At one point Sherry said to him, "Gee, Dad, I'm going to miss you so much". And his response was the best expression of the unknown that I have ever heard. He said, "I'll miss you too – if I can!"

The night Sam died, our daughters were with us, one of them on each side of him, holding his hands and talking and singing softly to him; I was able to sleep for a brief while in preparation for what I knew would be a difficult day ahead. I felt bad for Mark, who was running a national conference in Texas and was thus without the support which the girls and I were able to give one another.

Following the instructions I had been given, I phoned the funeral parlor immediately upon Sam's death, but assured the funeral director that he did not need to get his men up in the middle of the night. It could wait until morning. Though he came at once, he was very appreciative; he told me that nobody had ever before been concerned at disturbing him at night.

Sam died on a Sunday night, and the funeral was on Tuesday. On Monday afternoon I received a phone call from Rush Holt, the congressional representative from our district. We had supported him actively in all his campaigns, including running fund-raisers at our home, and he knew us well. He was due in Washington the next day, but would try to see if he could change plans so as to attend the funeral. I told him no; we had elected him to represent us in Washington, and respected his need to be there. Later, an aide called to ask if Rush could stop by for coffee that morning on his way to Washington. Just another example of the esteem in which Sam was held by all who knew him.

The funeral parlor was filled; I think there must have been three hundred people there. I made a firm decision that I would not allow this to be treated as a tragedy. A loss – a terrible loss! – yes. But when an eighty year old man dies, surrounded by loving family, after a rich and productive life, this cannot be counted a tragedy. Although I do not believe I had ever seen a widow giving the main eulogy for her husband, that was what I chose to do. Following is the text of what I wrote that day, and read at the funeral.

"We are assembled today to mourn the death of a very special man, someone who was universally loved. Look around you; you've come from all over the country to honor him. Phone calls have come from around the world – from France, from Japan, from Israel. This is a man who has made a difference in the lives of almost everyone he touched. And though this is a funeral and a farewell, we'd like it also to be a celebration of his life, a life which has made a difference not only to us who love him, but to the world in which he lived.

Sam's political activism on behalf of human rights, of civil rights, of women's rights, spanned over half a century. When we met 50 years ago – appropriately enough at a political workshop – he was already deeply involved in liberal politics, and we spent our courtship on a sound-truck for Adlai Stevenson. He wore the liberal label proudly, and it was a perspective which he applied to the many causes which he undertook. Whether it was as State Chairman of NJ Americans for Democratic Action; whether it was sharing the direction of the Cedar Grove Fair Housing Committee (which I started in our living room); whether it was speaking or writing or fundraising on behalf of citizen action, anti-war protests, or equal rights for women, Sam was always there – with his energy, with his creativity, with his well-reasoned and intelligent philosophy - a philosophy always seasoned with compassion. He lent his efforts to political candidates and campaigns as well, not only in support, but with suggestions to help shape their functioning. Even during his recent illness, he rose from his sickbed to lend his ideas and fundraising assistance to the Board of NJ Right To Choose.

An unmet need served as a clarion call for Sam. When we moved here seven years ago, he noted that there was no UJA-Federation section in Greenbriar /Whittingham. Where others might have bemoaned this lack, Sam got to work developing one. With his history as fund-raising chairman for UJA in Essex County, the Middlesex UJA is now tens of thousands richer because of his efforts.

Sam was a devoted family member. I don't just mean to his wife and children. I don't even just mean to his adored grandchildren – though five years ago he embarked on a third career as full-time grandfather. And I don't just mean to those in his original family. My parents were as dear to him as his own, and my brother became his. In fact, he often put me on notice: treat him right, or he would go home to my mother! We had an astonishingly large number of elderly relatives for whom to care, mostly childless aunts and uncles. Whether they were in New York or in Miami Beach, he always found the time to visit, to call, to encourage, and to help. And when my own mother began to decline, and we brought her out to live with us, I could never have cared for her so freely were it not for Sam's loving and tender sharing of the task.

Sam's was a truly open mind, reading and listening and learning until the last months of his life. Some of you may know that he went back to college after retiring, earning his bachelor's degree in 1997 – at the age of 74. There was no important issue of the day on which he did not try to integrate his understanding into his own belief system. And how he stood up for what he believed! We were in the stands to hear Martin Luther King's "I have a dream" speech. We were at every liberal march on Washington, whether for civil rights, for jobs and freedom, for women's rights, or to protest what we saw as an unjust war in Vietnam. Never pedantic or argumentative, he always spoke out for what he believed to be right, and his arguments were well-reasoned and persuasive.

When I was fifteen, and an early feminist, I wrote a song about him – eleven years before we met. It was a take-off on "The Girl That I Marry", and the central part about the man that I marry described him thus: "faithful and true as the stars up above; loyal and tender, sincere and kind, with a generous heart and a searching mind".

I could not describe him better today. The world will be a poorer place without him."

Of course, we sat *shiva* at my house, and both my Temple and the community arranged for nightly *minyans.* Sherry stayed on, of course, and Mark and Jess came each night with the children. On the first night, five year old Sol heard the prayers begin with "*Schmah,, Yisrael*", and his eyes lit up. "I know that one," he cried, and jumped from his seat to stand and recite it with the *minyan.* Every night after that, he insisted on coming along to "pray for Grandpa". Three year old Tessa was also desolate. Patting her stomach, she confided, "I miss Grandpa right here in my heart."

211

The grandchildren had been very close to Sam, and we wanted his memory to stay fresh with them. Jess got a new shrub, which they planted with great ceremony and which they called "the Grandpa bush". Also, perhaps with some confusion about his heavenly residence, the children watched for a star that might have Grandpa peeking over it. In addition to looking at his picture, they would often sing to me a ditty to the tune of The Farmer In The Dell, which Sam had made up when helping Sol to dress: "The belt goes on the pants; the belt goes on the pants; hi ho a derrio, the pants go on the belt ...no, no, no, the belt goes one the pants!" They found it hilarious.

Life without Sam was a very different experience. We had been so close that many people were, I believe, surprised that I did not seem more devastated. But that was just the point: we had been so close that I did not have the usual litany of regrets that assail so many of the recently bereaved. Nothing had been left unsaid; there were no "if only's", no "why didn't we's". We had done for each other everything that a loving couple could do, and while of course I missed him every day – and still do – I never felt that he had really left me. When I misplace something, I hear his calm voice saying, "When you get these papers cleared away, you'll find it." When I am struggling with a decision, I can give myself the advice which I know he would have offered. And perhaps most of all, we were always two separate people, not – as some romantics would have it – two halves of a whole. We did lots of things together, but we also did many things individually, so that my world continued on, even though its core was missing. And of course, my wonderful children and grandchildren, as well as friends and extended family, were always there for comfort and solace.

I was fortunate in having Mark and his family living near-by during those newly-widowed days. Some of the activities we shared laid the foundation for life-long memories. Cooking was one such, and when the children spent the night, we jointly made French toast for breakfast. The girls were so fond of cheese pie that when they came to dinner, almost the first words out of their mouths were, "Do we have cheese pie for dessert?" Of course, we made it together many times.

Also, one or both of the girls made cookies with me for various family Sedurim and Chanukah parties, proudly serving their productions themselves.

There was precedence for this baking. Many a rainy afternoon had been spent when my children were young, preparing and baking fancy cookies, decorated with raisins, chocolate chips, and often faces individually designed. In fact, Mark had once called me from college to arrange a major baking operation; he had not gotten a chance to buy Christmas and Chanukah gifts for his friends, and decided to bake several batches of cookies for that purpose. When I promised to have plenty of chocolate chips on hand, he demurred: he wanted to make the individually decorated cookies he remembered from his youth. Considering the time investment that would take, I also had the chocolate chips on hand, and Mark made both kinds.

As my arthritic knees began to make ground-level gardening difficult, Mother's Day became planting day for me, with one or more daughter and daughter-in-law plus two granddaughters putting in my annuals. I recall that Tessa planted marigolds around my front tree, while Sasha specialized in helping her Auntie Robin with the border begonias. And what of Mark and Sol, you may ask? Both quite uninterested in gardening, they played ball in the back yard!

213

Although Sol didn't share my love of cooking and gardening, there certainly were other things which we enjoyed together. From infancy on I had read to him, and have been delighted to see him following family tradition in his enjoyment of poetry. He also possesses a quick, inquiring mind, and when he was perhaps eight or nine I found an Intergenerational Elder Hostel which I thought he would enjoy. It was a week of "discovery" based at the Boston Museum of Science, with hotel accommodations nearby. They had special programs planned just for our group, and Sol and I spent an exciting week there together. I think of those days every time I visit that museum. Sol, like the others, also loved the Museum of Natural History in New York. Taking him there was reminiscent of my own childhood days, when my mother used to take us to that very museum. And my nephew Wes has similar happy memories.

I wanted to have similar experiences with the girls, and searched the Elder Hostel catalogues for ideas. Unable to find anything appropriate for such a young age, I suggested to Tessa that we spend a long weekend in New York; as she is interested in theatre, I thought we could take in a couple of shows, eat in interesting restaurants and generally make an occasion of it. She declined; could she spend a weekend with me, baking, instead? So that is what we did. And alas, I can no longer meet the walking requirements that Elder Hostel sets up for these intergenerational trips, so I cannot offer the same option to Sasha.

In the course of any life, there are good times and bad; if we are lucky, the former outnumber the latter. I have certainly been fortunate in that regard. Among other memories I think of the lavish party which Jess gave for Mark's fiftieth birthday. It was creative in the extreme, photographic history and all, and there were family and friends from every phase of Mark's life. We were all invited to say a few words about Mark; this is what I presented:

"There is so much to say about Mark - where to begin?
Well -It was clear from early days that Mark was destined to be an entrepreneur. Two examples come to mind.

When he was about 8, he went into the car-washing business with his younger sister and a friend. After a while, I came out to see how the business was going. Robin and Joe were elbow deep in suds and water, scrubbing away with gusto. Mark, clean and dry, was handling the money, taking orders, and generally running the enterprise. It was a dead giveaway of things to come.

The summer following Mark's first year of college, he got himself a factory job, packaging toothbrushes. He lasted about two days before he quit, feeling he would go mad with the monotony of it. Yet, how to earn money for day-to-day expenses at college? He obtained a license from the town, bought paint and a stencil, and went door-to-door offering to paint house numbers on the curb. At a dollar a pop, he was doing so well that he increased his price to two dollars, and later to three. I heard the following story from my neighbor, who had a friend on the next block: Her teenage daughter answered the door, heard Mark's spiel, and went to get her mother. "Mom," she breathed, "I don't know what it is he's selling, but whatever it is, buy it. He has the most gorgeous blue eyes!" So, as you can see, his entrepreneurial path lay clear!

Mark has always had the gift of making others feel comfortable. An early example: at his eighth birthday party he was given one of those little collectible cars, identical to the one he had just unwrapped. As I mentally scrambled to think of a way to soothe the giver's feelings, Mark's face lit up. "Oh, good!" he said. Now I have two of them, so they can play with each other!"

Mark was a fairly late talker (a situation which has surely been more than remedied in the ensuing years) and Sam, limited in his experience with young children, had only his super-early-talking daughter as a reference point. One morning I saw him watching Mark at play. Shaking his head sadly, he said, "He's such a sweet little boy. What a shame he's never going to be smart like Sherry." Outraged, I declared, "When he graduates from college, I'm going to tell him you said that!" And when he graduated from Wesleyan Magna Cum Laude (or was it Summa?) - I did!

Did you know that Mark was an inventor at a very early age? When he was around nine or ten, perhaps having heard discussion among his mother and sisters relating to dieting, he announced that he was going to invent a new kind of scale. Usually, when you step on the scale, it registers what you weigh. With his scale, you set it to the weight you want to be, and when you step on it, your body adjusts to the scale's setting. Trying to contain my excitement and aware of the Law of Conservation of Matter, I asked what would happen to all the extra poundage now contained in the scale. Without missing a beat, this grandson of a pediatrician replied, "You know how mothers are always complaining about their babies not gaining enough weight? I'd just sell the extra weight to them!" Of course, I reminded him that I was his mother, and as such entitled to the first model off the assembly line!

Mark was always able to con his sisters. I'll pass over how he convinced them to pool their birthday or Chanukah gift money to buy something in which only he was interested. But even in their teens, he had them convinced that washing dishes was evenly divided if they did the work while he entertained them by playing his accordion. It was reminiscent of an earlier time, when he could not go out to play until his bed was made- and his sympathetic sisters made it for him, and were indignant that I did not consider this a satisfactory solution. (I told them that we each did our own chores around here, and I was not raising helpless people.) Clearly, if Mark had not had such a mean Mommy, he might have grown up to be a con man, instead of the thoughtful, generous, caring man we honor today! Happy Birthday, Mark."

CHAPTER XXX: AN END AND A BEGINNING

I had a good support system in Greenbriar, with many friends and activities, and my life continued active and full. After a while, however, Mark and his family moved back to California, so that my nearest children were a goodly distance away. Sam and I had decided long ago, with our experience of caring for elderly relatives, that when we grew old we would move near to one of our children. We did not want them to feel the need to drop everything and come running any time one of us was sick. If we needed financial supervision, as did my mother and some of Sam's aunts and uncles, it would be easier for them if we were nearby. At this point the children were urging me to consider such a move, and I began to explore my possibilities. Despite the lure of being near my grandchildren, I did not want to move to California – all my friends and other family were on the east coast. With Sherry in the Boston area, this seemed a good locale to consider. I still had friends here from graduate school, and as an extra bonus, Wes and his family live in nearby New Hampshire. And for Robin the distance was about the same to Boston as to New Jersey.

Over the course of a year I visited a number of Independent Living facilities. Having grown up in an apartment, as well as seeing Mother's satisfactory experience at Kittay House, I was readily able to accept the whole concept. I think my major area of reluctance was at the thought of living somewhere that Sam had never been. But I knew that I would carry him with me wherever I chanced to lodge; no way could I ever lose that!

Wherever I visited, I didn't settle for the residents chosen for me by the administration; I wandered the halls, speaking to people at random. And at any place which interested me I arranged to have a meal. Although there were some places nearer to Sherry's home, I chose Cabot Park Village in Newtonville. I had a good feeling about both the residents and the staff, the latter seeming especially warm and kind. It was clear that I would find people here with whom I could develop friendly relationships, and the range of available activities was satisfyingly broad. I met Sylvia, the editor of the quarterly news magazine here, and she suggested I write an article about my visit. It was printed in the next issue. Here it is:

Musings of a Prospective Resident
By Sarai Zitter

It's been a visit to remember! Was it in only two days that I was so graciously wined (by Betty) and dined (by Sylvia)? Housed in such a bright and roomy apartment? Introduced to so many of the amenities and comforts of Cabot Park Village?

Each of us has lived long enough to face the question – to move or not to move. Each of us has dealt with similar issues: Am I getting tired of household chores? or conversely, can I bear to give up my comfortable, spacious, and most of all familiar home? Will I find new friends, a new support system, to help compensate for being so far from those I now trust and love? Will there be activities which I enjoy, and which contribute to my continuing the interesting and meaningful life which I now experience? For some, nearness to a particular religious institution may be of importance; for others, the potential for political or social service. For many of us, nearness to one or more of our children factors in.

In the past year I have visited quite a number of Independent Living facilities. I had already settled on Cabot Park as my first choice, when I learned of the opportunity to visit. From a mere intellectual concept, the possibility of living here has become internalized as a valid expectation. The physical facilities are laid out to feel comfortable and homey, with everything well-appointed, well-maintained and clean. The food was excellent, and as a non-meat-eater I appreciate the always-available alternative menu. There were activities available both on and off campus in which I participated, and I could see that there was freedom to become involved in off-grounds activities as well. Knowing Newton, for instance, I'm sure I could find a League of Women Voters chapter nearby. Of course, having this newsletter also offers an opportunity to continue my lifelong pleasure in writing. The staff was uniformly warm and friendly; it was clear that everyone shared the goal of making this a comfortable and satisfying stay.

Most of all, however, were the residents, who so graciously hosted me. I was invited to various apartments and encouraged to try various activities. Their warmth and enthusiasm would surely make for a welcoming and happy atmosphere. And I enjoyed the beautiful grounds, including raised beds wherein I, a gardening enthusiast, could continue my love-affair with the soil without damage to my aging knees.

And so back to the crucial question: to move or not to move? It is clear to me that, when I do, it will be to Cabot Park Village. This may not be a good time to sell a house. This may not be a good time to go from a mortgage-free home with minimum maintenance costs to a facility with so many additional services, but of course at additional cost as well. And yet, as I approach my eighty-third birthday, I remember the famous question of Rabbi Hillel, which I have always thought of as my personal mantra: if not now, when?"

Just before I moved to Cabot Park Village, we had another great occasion to celebrate. Sherry and Sarah, taking advantage of the same-sex marriage laws in Massachusetts, joined their lives. The wedding was held outdoors at the lovely home of Sarah's mother. The two brides were, of course, beautiful and the service – conducted by their friend Reye and Sarah's sister Susan – was lovely. We were so delighted to welcome Sarah into the family, and it is a joy to me to see how well all the siblings and their spouses get along together. They make major efforts to see one another, despite the distances involved, and I am happy frequently to be involved in their plans. Sherry and Sarah were planning to buy a new home, and questioned if I might like to join them. I was inordinately touched by the invitation, but felt I would be too isolated during the day, not to mention a burden on their privacy.

I was invited to offer the final blessings for the couple, and what I said is reproduced below. If much of it sounds familiar from Heather and Jesse's wedding, it is because my core beliefs about a healthy marriage remain intact. I might add that Sarah, an artist, designed and created the most beautiful Ketubah I have ever seen. The wording was both original and very appropriate to their particular situation, and the artwork included delightful touches related to their individual heritages.

Sarai G. Zitter

Blessings for Sarah and Sherry – Wedding

"I knew when I was awarded this position that I would be following such a wealth of loving good wishes that I would find very little left unsaid. And so, claiming parental privilege, I'd like to tell you what I think are the blessings of a happy marriage – and you will know that these are what I so warmly wish for you. Although each relationship is unique, there are a few commonalities that I think we find in most successful unions

Love is surely basic – and is the very reason we are here. And today your love moves to a new level – that of commitment. There is an important difference between courtship and marriage. In the former, one may see a problem and wonder if you will be able to solve it. In the latter, the question is how you will solve it; commitment means that you know you will, you must, find a way.

Respect – easy when we see eye to eye, but perhaps more demanding when our experiences, our preferences or tastes lead us in different directions. No two people will agree on everything. You, Sherry and Sarah, come with two separate lifetimes of experiences and preferences. But you know how to disagree without being disagreeable – and I know that your respectful, courteous listening is one of the things which helps each of you to feel comfortable with your eventual decisions. And my wish for you is the continuation of the many, many ways in which you do see eye to eye, and share your concerns and goals. Today's wedding, with its emphasis on concern for the earth and all its inhabitants, future as well as present, is a shining example of the kind of caring and sharing which keeps a marriage always fresh and interesting.

A loving relationship makes it possible to admit mistakes and disappointments with the expectation of support rather than criticism. In this, your home becomes a true haven from the many stresses of the world. There is a magical mathematics to this – while a burden shared is thereby diminished, a triumph shared becomes bigger and brighter. And of course, the whole – the marriage, the relationship – is greater than the sum of its parts.

Some marriages pride themselves on constant togetherness – the notion of two people merging into one. I think the richest of relationships, however, are those in which two people do not merge, but continue to bless one another with the individuality and uniqueness which first attracted them to one another. And so, my wish for you is that you each retain your own sense of self, and do not let caring for one another diminish the importance of caring also for yourselves.

And of course, every happy marriage includes a sense of fun. Laughter has been found to be good for your health – but I've noticed that it's good for marriage, too. A little humor can lighten many a dark moment, and laughter can frequently defuse tense ones.

My wish for you both, Sherry and Sarah, is that your union may enlarge you, encourage growth in each of you. And I have a prediction, too: if you think your beloved is terrific now, just wait a while. As you grow and your relationship matures, I can assure you that this perception will only be enhanced by the passing years.

Let me close with what is known as the three-fold blessing of the Torah, adapted for this occasion:

Sarai G. Zitter

May Shahina bless you and keep you.
May Shahina cause Her countenance to shine upon you.
May Shahina be gracious unto you, and grant you peace.

As not everyone could be invited to the wedding, we had a reception at my home for those in my area who had not been included. It was to be the last gathering I had in Monroe Township before moving, and I took the greatest pleasure in being able to plan and execute the event.

CHAPTER XXXI: MY LAST HOME

It has been a year and a half now since I moved to Cabot Park Village. I have a large, bright apartment with rooms spacious enough that I can use my bedroom also as a den, while enough of my old furniture fits in the living room so that from the first I have felt very much at home. My predictions have proven to be correct; there are many people here with whom I have become friendly, and a few with whom I have developed a real friendship. The staff is kind and helpful, and with all the services provided, I find it to be real luxury living. Being me, of course I've gotten involved in many activities. I've been chair of the Gardening Committee, responsible for planting and maintaining the three raised beds which so attracted me when I visited. I'm on our Ombudsman Committee, helping negotiate issues between residents and management. I've served on the Nominating Committee and I sing in the chorus. But most important of all, I've been active on the Chronicle, our quarterly news magazine. I progressed quickly from writing to serving as co-editor, and have just graduated to editor in the most recent issue. It's been both my pleasure and my privilege to work with Sylvia Lehrich, the woman who brought it from a few pages stapled together to the beautiful published issue it has become. I am fortunate to have her continued assistance with the Chronicle, and even more so to have her friendship.

My neighbors tease me that I live here only part time, as I have had so many occasions to be gone for a few days, sometimes even a week or more. One such major occasion was Sol's recent Bar Mitzvah, surely one of the most special occasions a grandmother could enjoy. He was thoroughly prepared, and led the entire service with obvious expertise.

He even made a special effort to slow down his speech, so that I might understand it. Not only his poise, but his warmth and enthusiasm were a pleasure to behold. It has whet my appetite for the two Bat Mitzvahs soon to come. I appreciated the special privilege of giving Sol his *tallith*, and hope I can negotiate the same opportunity in regard to Tessa and Sasha.

In addition to the ceremony itself, we had a weekend of celebration. At the dinner party at night, many of us were invited to offer toasts to Sol. I was given the privilege of being first, and offered the following:

Solomon's thirteen years, almost;
As his Grammy, I've got the right to boast.
There's so many things that are special about him.
A poorer world it would be without him.

You can count on his word – what he says, is true.
You can count on his always helping, too.
An inquiring mind he has as well,
For all that this wide world has to tell.

Talk about caring for those in need –
Sol is the first one up to speed.
His heart's as big as his soccer ball!
Generosity, kindness, he shows to all.

My grandson Sol is simply great!
I'll say it early, I'll say it late.
So reaching this auspicious date,
We know it's time to celebrate.

What about simply having fun?
For a great companion, he's the one!
So to Solomon Zitter, here's a toast:
As a friend and a grandson, he's the most!

TO SOL!

Like every grandmother, I think my grandchildren are special. They share many qualities – all are bright, articulate, loving and fun to be with. They all have friends and they all enjoy a variety of activities. Though they share a love for animals, Sasha seems to have a special affinity for them, and at one time was the youngest volunteer at an animal shelter, playing with the puppies and kittens to help socialize them for later adoption. For Tessa, the powerful draw is toward performance – singing, dancing and acting – and her strong and well-modulated voice is reminiscent of Sherry at that age. I am glad she is getting the training and experience she so much enjoys. I might add that she has had parts in performances well beyond school, and seems on her way to success in an area which will give her lifelong satisfaction. Both girls have enjoyed cooking and baking with me whenever possible, and Tessa at one point started learning to knit. I hope she continues to enjoy that skill, which has given me such pleasure throughout the years. And both girls show some artistic promise – an ability which never fails to astound me, as I have absolutely none. But they come by it honestly; Sam was quite artistic (when we sent greeting cards, I would supply the verse and he would decorate the card!) and his uncle was a professional artist. My Aunt Mollie also had some skill in that area.

In that context, I might mention our birth announcements. Sam designed them, and we set them up as a mystery book series. Sherry began as Volume 1, The Case of The New Arrival; Mark was Volume 2 as The Case of The Next of Kin, while Robin weighed in with Volume 3, The Case of the Third Part Harmony. The usual statistics were identified as clues.

Sol's talents lie elsewhere. He enjoys sports – has been on soccer and swim teams, and is studying fencing at present – and has an excellent singing voice (in both Hebrew and English). I know he loves electronics, and I take him at his word about his ability with computers; he uses the name "Technowhiz" for his email. His skill with a camera showed itself in publications of his school newspaper. He is also quite protective of me, taking my arm on stairs and when the dark makes my balance uncertain. He used to share his room with me when he was younger, and when I thanked him, would assure me it was fine – "We're roomies." All the children are warm and loving, and I count myself very fortunate indeed to have them.

I have other occasions to be away from home. Bat Mitzvahs, Bar Mitzvahs, weddings – they are only the beginning. I still go to New York occasionally, staying with Mollie and visiting with other friends and family in the area. I go to Long Island for the extended family's annual Father's Day party at Judi and Lee's. I go to camp each summer with my cousin Helen Topf, and Mollie comes with us. Helene joined us last year, but will not be able to make it this time. I haven't mentioned some of the other trips I've taken. I took a river boat cruise with Helen through the Russian waterways, from St. Petersburg to Moscow. I went to the Greek Islands with Flip (though she likes it warm and I like it cold, she likes to sleep late and I'm an early riser, we somehow manage to room together with great delight!) And I have been to the British Isles with Sherry twice, once to Noah Miller's Bar Mitzvah, and again on a trip to Scotland and Wales. I shall include here a copy of the article I wrote about the latter trip.

THE GREAT BOTANIC GARDEN ESCAPE!
by Sarai Zitter

I recently returned from a trip to Wales, accompanied by my daughter. Like all trips, it was a wonderful experience – hiking along the cliffs, visiting museums and craft centers, wool factories and collections of unusual animals – but a real high spot was our visit to the new Welch National Botanic Gardens.

Having gotten lost, we arrived somewhat late in the day; in fact, it was 4:30, and they were officially closing at that time. But the receptionist welcomed us warmly and encouraged us to stay and see what we could in the next hour and a half, at which time they actually would be closing. So, we asked, we must be back by six? Reassuringly, she told us we had ten or fifteen minutes of leeway.

When we got back to the entrance at about 6:02, everything was locked up tight. Gates were secured, doors were locked, and no way out presented itself. No public phones – everyone there uses cell phones, and ours were not functional in Europe. The Gardens were way out of town, on a dead-end street – no reason to expect a passerby who might hear and rescue us.

We examined our options. The greenhouses were unlocked, and probably maintained their temperature at night. Of course, they were also pretty high in humidity. Hmm. Probably not the best place to sleep. Could we scale the fence? One gate had horizontal wooden slats; would it serve as a ladder? Closer inspection showed one slat broken, and the next one creaked and sagged when I tested it with my foot. Clearly we could not trust our weight to it. The other gate consisted of vertical metal rods; no place to rest a foot.

Seeking something to use as a step, we unearthed a shed of electric wheelchairs. However, were we to use one, it would remain out all night – and Wales seems to have rain every few hours. Finally, we found a couple of cafeteria chairs, and the problem was solved. We heaved one over the top of the gate to receive a descending foot, and set the other on the near side as a step. Voila. My daughter was treated to the sight of her then seventy-eight year old, arthritic mother scaling the barrier in what was probably the first attempt anyone ever made to break OUT of the National Botanic Garden.

And we have pictures to prove it!

I have spoken about the many family gatherings we have always enjoyed. Though most of us love them, Robin has always tended to avoid crowds, and is not always in attendance. However, there is one holiday which she so enjoys that in our family it has become hers – Thanksgiving. There is something very appropriate in this; she provides most of the dinner from her own vegetable garden, supplemented by items brought by her guests.

Robin is vegan, as are Sherry and Sarah, and some people have asked me what there is to eat if there is no turkey. I wrote an article about that for the Chronicle; it appears below.

A VEGAN THANKSGIVING
Sarai Zitter

A friend once asked my son, "How does it feel to have a sister who is a lesbian?" His reply: "That's nothing. My other sister is a vegetarian!" In fact, both my daughters were then vegetarians, from which they progressed to being vegan. The difference? A vegetarian eats nothing that had a mother – meat, fish, poultry. A vegan additionally eats nothing that is the product of something that had a mother – ie., eggs, milk, and all dairy foods. (It's much harder to cook and bake for vegans!)

My younger daughter Robin, a professional horticulturist, hosts our Thanksgiving feast, and much of what we eat is from her garden. However, each of us brings a favorite dish or two, and we rise from the table more than sated. People keep asking me what we serve, if there is no turkey. Well, how about these dishes: Garlicky homemade hummus; corn salsa; eggplant dip; pumpkin seed pate; seasoned raw young asparagus; tamari-roasted almonds; tamarind sauce; an Indian pate made of almonds, sunflower seeds, red peppers, sun-dried tomatoes, cumin and curry; pomegranate; and of course crudités, mostly from Robin's garden, and including such unexpected items as daikon, rutabaga, and turnip – all served with flatbread, multigrain crackers and baked chips. And these were just the appetizers!

While we nosh, the children – aided by some of the more artistic adults – are creating centerpieces out of odd or interesting vegetable matter which Robin has collected. Thus, a bushy carrot top can become a peacock's tail, and a multi-legged parsnip gets a face. The "animals" get weirder by the year, while toothpicks and raisins flow with abandon.

The main course always begins with a choice of soups (this time it was hot and sour or potato leek) and many of us try both. Main courses included nut loaf with miso-mushroom gravy; sweet and sour satay with coconut oil dressing; roasted root veggies, including red and white beets; steamed mixed greens; baked coconut squash; and a complete stalk of Brussels sprouts, seasoned, roasted and served on the stalk. Of course there were relishes (cranberry–orange and chutney), cole slaw, and homemade bread and cornbread. Is it any wonder that most of us took a walk before dessert?

Ah, dessert. I put on pounds just remembering them. Apple pie, brownies, and hot fruit crisp were upstaged by an incredible pumpkin tofu 'cheese' cake, all enjoyed with coffee, tea, and hot chocolate for the children. (Did I forget to mention the vegan macaroons, home-made biscotti, non-dairy ice-cream and glazed roasted chestnuts?) As the last of the wine was imbibed, and the last of the left-overs parceled out or stored, we were already discussing possible menus for next year's Thanksgiving feast.

I should add that Robin is no longer doing the Thanksgiving entertaining alone. She has been sharing her life with a warm and thoughtful man named Mike, and they have just bought a large parcel of land together. It is 54 acres; I must say that I never expected to have landed gentry in the family. But we are all delighted to welcome Mike as one of us. He doesn't join just Robin; he also joins her three cats and a dog, to which another dog has been added since his arrival. All in all, they comprise quite a large family. (That seems to run in the family. Sherry and Sarah have, at last count, two dogs and a cat.)

AFTERWORD

I have now been settled in Cabot Park Village for about a year and a half. Do I miss my former home? Of course; there is no way to leave friends behind without missing them. But am I pleased and satisfied to have made the move? Absolutely! I have made good friends, I have satisfying activities, I stay in touch with the friends and family whom I love, and my needs are met with kindness and caring. When I want privacy, I shut the door to my apartment and achieve it. When I want company, I go downstairs and find it within my community. And best of all, I am only half an hour from Sherry and Sarah, who include me in many of their activities. I sometimes join Sherry at a meeting, and she sometimes stops by for dinner on her way to Boston. We often drive together to family gatherings. Robin's visits vary by the growing season – more in mid-summer and dead of winter, pretty much absent during the spring and fall. And in addition to planned family visits, Mark is sometimes in Boston on business, so that I get to see him then.

I also have Wes and Laurie nearby – just about an hour and a half away – and have been able to watch Emily at her exciting new hobby of sled dog racing. Julia lives nearby, as do Heather's parents-in-law, so I also get to see Heather and Jesse when they come east. And at this very moment, Ashley and her fiancé Matt are staying with me for a few days while they find housing; Matt has a new job in Newton, and Ashley has just found one in Lexington.

I once read that one should not say, at life's end, that life has been good to me; rather, say that I have been good to life. I like to think that I can say both. Life certainly has been and continues to be good to me. I hope that I have made contributions which have made me good to life as well. And I hope that my grandchildren, reading this memoir, can have the good fortune to be able to say the same.

A memoir must be, by definition, unfinished. I have written of where I have been but cannot know for certain where the vicissitudes of life will next carry me, nor what I shall do with the time remaining to me. I suppose that, if it is indeed ever completed, that task will fall to one of my children. I can only hope that it may go something like this:

"Mother lived out her remaining years in the comfort and pleasure of her latest home, Cabot Park Village near Boston, Massachusetts. She remained active in affairs of her community, espousing and working for the same causes which had engaged her attention throughout her life. Her editorship of the Cabot Park Chronicle, through very demanding of time and effort, gave her considerable satisfaction. She continued to enjoy visits from her children and grandchildren, from whose love and support she derived the greatest pleasure.

With her mental capacities still intact, she died peacefully at home, surrounded by her beloved family."

I hope I shall be fortunate enough for that to be true. But in any event, I am grateful for my already-long life, enriched by loving family and friends and blessed by fifty years spent with a truly remarkable man. My only regret is that so many exciting things will be going on in the future - and I'll be missing out on them……….

Would you like to see your manuscript become a book?

If you are interested in becoming a PublishAmerica author, please submit your manuscript for possible publication to us at:

acquisitions@publishamerica.com

You may also mail in your manuscript to:

**PublishAmerica
PO Box 151
Frederick, MD 21705**

www.publishamerica.com

CPSIA information can be obtained at www.ICGtesting.com
Printed in the USA
BVOW020652141011

273585BV00001B/4/P